D0262952

TwinPack
Sicily

SALLY ROY

Sally Roy has known and loved Italy for many years, travelling throughout the country researching every aspect of its history, art, architecture and countryside. She is the author of the AA Key Guide to Venice, the main contributor to Key Guide Italy, Florence and Tuscany and Rome, and has written Spiral Guides, Essential Guides and Citypacks to all areas of Italy.

If you have any comments or suggestions for this guide you can contact the editor at *Twinpacks@theAA.com*

AA Publishing
Find out more about AA Publishing and the wide range of travel publications and services the AA provides by visiting our website at *www.theAA.com/travel*

Contents

life *5–12*

how to organise your time *13–22*

top 25 sights *23–48*

About this book

KEY TO SYMBOLS

✚ Grid reference to the Top 25 locator map

✉ Address

☎ Telephone number

🕐 Opening times

🍴 Restaurant or café on premises or nearby

Ⓜ Nearest underground (tube) station

🚊 Nearest railway station

🚌 Nearest bus route

⛴ Nearest riverboat or ferry stop

♿ Facilities for visitors with disabilities

✋ Admission charge

↔ Other nearby places of interest

❓ Tours, lectures or special events

► Indicates the page where you will find a fuller description

ℹ Tourist information

TwinPack Sicily is divided into six sections to cover the six most important aspects of your visit to the region. It includes:

- The author's view of Sicily and its people
- Suggested walks and drives
- The Top 25 Sights to visit
- The best of the rest – aspects of Sicily that make it special
- Detailed listings of restaurants, hotels, shops and nightlife
- Practical information

In addition, easy-to-read side panels provide fascinating extra facts and snippets, highlights of places to visit and invaluable practical advice.

CROSS-REFERENCES
To help you make the most of your visit, cross-references, indicated by ► , show you where to find additional information about a place or subject.

MAPS
The fold-out map in the wallet at the back of the book is a large-scale map of Sicily.
The Top 25 locator maps found on the inside front cover and inside back cover of the book itself are for quick reference. They show the Top 25 Sights, described on pages 24–48, which are clearly plotted by number (**1** – **25** , not page number) in alphabetical order.

PRICES
Where appropriate, an indication of the cost of an attraction is given by 🏛 Expensive, Moderate or Inexpensive. An indication of the cost of a restaurant is given by € signs: €€€ denotes higher prices, €€ denotes average prices, while € denotes lower prices.

SICILY
life

A Personal View

SEEING SICILY

If you want to explore Sicily properly you should think of car rental during your stay. Public transport can be slow and routes complicated, and some of what you'll want to see may be far from towns or railway stations. If you do drive, it's best not to attempt to drive into either Palermo or Catania, and be extra vigilant on the road at all times – Sicilian drivers have a style all of their own.

At the heart of the Mediterranean, at the cross-roads of east and west, north and south, the island of Sicily sits like some jewel in the sea. Part of Italy, but detached from it by a few kilometres of water, it's an island apart, with a unique history, culture and way of life. For some visitors it's a holiday playground, where the sun shines from a cloudless sky on to perfect sands and clear blue water, for others it's a treasure trove of art, architecture and history, while others again journey here to pursue special interests such as bird-watching, walking, music, eating and drinking. The chances are your experience will be far richer than you could have ever imagined.

It's the contrasts that first hit home. Leave the developed coastal resorts and head inland and you enter a different world, where the land is sweeping and empty, scattered with secretive villages locked in the dusty torpor and lassitude of what is still one of Italy's poorest regions. Inland Sicily is still undiscovered, a beautiful landscape of rolling hills and high mountains, astoundingly green in spring, baked and bleached of colour in the searing summer heat. The silent, shuttered villages of the interior are a world away from the noisy, crowded markets of Palermo and the big towns, with their vibrant colours, enticing scents and jostling, hustling crowds.

There's no doubt Sicilians can be noisy, living life to the full, their emotions out in the open for all to see. But they're warm-hearted to an overwhelming degree, friendly and outgoing, proud of their island and its heritage. Centuries of invasion made them a mongrel people, with Greek, Arab, Norman and Spanish blood in their veins, making them very different from the stereotypical Italian image. Their history cursed them

Handsome Castelbuono is capital of the Madonie

with the Mafia, but Sicilians today are increasingly facing the problems of the *piovra* (octopus) in their midst, and there's a definite sense of changing times. Young people no longer flee the island, preferring to stay and build their lives at home, and there's no doubt that Sicilians are more prosperous. The awful poverty has gone, and, despite continued high unemployment, the standard of living continues to rise. Attitudes are more open, the atmosphere more relaxed, political life less introverted. Sicilians are learning to face the future and celebrate the richness, not the drawbacks, of their heritage.

This heritage is everywhere in the island's wonderful monuments – the great classical sites with their temples as fine as anything in Greece, the Roman villas, the Norman cathedrals and the extravagant baroque churches. You'll see it in Sicily's towns and cities, where Byzantine mosaics are set among Norman French architecture, warrens of streets recall the souks of north Africa and whole towns look like extravagant stage sets waiting for the curtain to rise. You'll sense it in the huge countryside estates, where peasant farmers are unknown and one family owns the land as far as you can see in all directions. You'll experience it in the emotion of the great feast days, both sad and joyful, with their processions and religious fervour. Above all, you'll taste it in Sicilian cooking, its colour, flavour and heat the legacy of all the past invaders, savour it in the incredible variety of sugary treats and luscious ices, drink it down in wines as rich and dark as any in the world.

Scratch the surface and Sicily has layer upon layer beneath, and it's this that brings her myriad fans back to the island again and again.

SEEING THE SIGHTS

If you're visiting in summer, plan your sightseeing carefully. Many of the archaeological sites are very exposed and are unbearably hot in the middle of the day, and you should also remember that museums and churches normally close for 2–3 hours during the siesta time.

Ornate architecture and glittering mosaics are breathtaking sights

Sicily in Figures

GEOGRAPHY

- Sicily covers an area of 24,807sq km (9,923sq miles).
- Sicily lies 3km (1.8 miles) off the southwest 'toe' of Italy with Malta 93km (58 miles) and north Africa 150km (98 miles) to the south.
- It is surrounded by the Ionian Sea to the east, the Tyrrenian Sea to the north and the Mediterranean to the south and west.
- Sicily has three offshore island groups, the Eolie to the north, the Egadi to the west and the Pelagie to the south, and two separate islands, Pantelleria to the south and Ustica to the north.
- Mount Etna is 3,323m (10,902 feet) high.
- The Madonie mountains are 1,970m (6,462 feet) high.
- Tourism is a major contributor to the economy.

CLIMATE

- The average daily temperatures are 28°C (82°F) in summer and 12°C (54°F) in winter.
- Winter generally lasts between December and February.
- Weather in the interior mountains can be much colder than on the coast, with snow and frost at high altitudes.
- Rainfall is mainly confined to November, December and January.
- During summer, the *scirocco*, a hot wind from Africa, can blow for days at a time.

AGRICULTURE

- Sicily's main agricultural produce is wheat, citrus fruit, grapes and olives.
- Sicily produces early vegetable and fruit crops for distribution throughout Italy.
- Pistachio nuts, mulberries, prickly pears and capers are important local agricultural products.
- Sheep and cattle are bred for meat and milk.
- Historic crops include sugar cane and cotton.
- Sicily has more than 200 plant species unique to the island.

People of Sicily

King Roger II

Born in 1095, Roger was the son of Roger I, first Norman ruler of Sicily. Well-educated and cosmopolitan, he became ruler in 1105, extending his power to southern Italy by 1144 and being crowned King of Sicily in 1130. During his reign, Palermo (the Arab Bal'harm) emerged as one of the wealthiest royal capitals of Europe and the Mediterranean, and Sicily was characterised by its multi-ethnic nature, religious tolerance and enlightened government. Roger supported scholarship and learning, publishing his legal documents in Greek, Latin and Arabic and entertaining intellectuals. He supported art and architecture, and many of Sicily's greatest buildings survive from his age. He married three times, his eldest son, William I, reigning at his side from 1150 to 1154, the year of his death.

Count Alessandro Cagliostro

Charlatan, imposter, conman and alchemist, Cagliostro was born Giuseppe Balsamo in Palermo in 1743. He started a spree of forgery, hooking up with the ravishing Lorenza Feliciani in Rome, where the couple embarked on a career of magic, their alchemy and mysticism thrilling the aristocracy all over Europe. By 1771 Giuseppe had assumed the title of Count Cagliostro and was claiming an orphaned past, noble parentage and an education in magic. Finally unmasked in London in 1785, he was deserted by Lorenza and, back in Italy, locked up for life. Quite insane, he died in 1795.

Luigi Pirandello

Born in Agrigento in 1867, Pirandello's work as a playwright, obsessed with the illusory nature of existence and the isolation of man, foreshadows that of Samuel Becket and Harold Pinter. This disillusionment stemmed from personal tragedy; he was married to a young woman who suffered a complete nervous collapse, which led to 17 years of violence, during which time her husband cared for her at home. His masterpiece is *Six Characters in Search of an Author* and he was awarded the Nobel Prize for Literature in 1934.

Bust of Luigi Pirandello in Giardino Inglese, Palermo

9

A Chronology

35,000–9000BC	Palaeolithic era
6000–1200BC	Agricultural societies of Sikans, Elymians and Sikels emerge; first potters at work
735BC	First Greek settlers arrive on east coast
650–580BC	Selinunte, Agrigento and Siracusa established; Phoenicians from Carthage establish colonies on west coast
5th-3rd century BC	Greek Golden Age
397BC	Phoenicians expelled by Greeks
AD264–AD261	Second Punic War heralds start of Roman occupation
270–410	Rome exploits Sicily for grain and slaves; latifundia system established
5TH CENTURY	Goths and Vandals occupy Sicily
535	Start of 300 years of Byzantine rule
827	Muslim invasion from north Africa. Start of new Golden Age as Arabs introduce new farming methods. Palermo becomes cosmopolitan and cultured capital
1040	Norman mercenaries arrive from southern Italy; Roger de Hauteville moves against Muslims
1091	Roger de Hauteville takes all Sicily and is proclaimed Roger I. Palermo remains one of Mediterranean's richest cities
1091–1189	Norman Kingdom of Sicily, third Golden Age
1198–1250	Sicily ruled as part of Holy Roman Empire by Frederick Hohenstaufen II; remains prosperous and stable
1282	War of the Vespers; Peter III of Aragon becomes King of Sicily

1291–1720	Spanish rule in Sicily; Sicily systematically impoverished
1669	Eruption of Etna destroys most of Catania
1693	Earthquake kills at least 50,000
1720	Bourbons established as rulers
1848	Abortive uprising for unity starts in Palermo
1860	Giuseppe Garibaldi lands in Marsala, takes Palermo, declares Sicily part of new Italy
1866–1890	Emergence of socialist fasci movement; this was to evolve into the Mafia
1908	Messina earthquake kills 80,000
1890–1920	Emigration; around 25 per cent of the population leave Sicily
1930–1939	Mussolini cracks down on Mafia
1939	World War II begins
1943	Allies invade Europe via Sicily; Mafia lend their expertise and regain their power
1947	First meeting of Sicilian Regional Parliament
1950–1970	Further economic emigration. Some industrial development
1970	Start of campaign against Mafia heralds start of murders and *maxiprocessi* (trials) in 1980s
1992	Prosecutors Giovanni Falcone and Paolo Borsellino killed by Mafia car bomb
1995	Mafia trials and arrests continue
2005	Prime Minister Berlusconi announces plan for bridge across the Straits of Messina
2006	Prime Minister Prodi cancels bridge

Best of Sicily

*There's plenty to tempt
sweet-toothed visitors*

If you have only a short time to visit Sicily, or would like to get a complete picture of the island, here are the essentials:

- See some of the great Norman buildings and their glittering mosaics by visiting Palermo (➤ 14) or Cefalù (➤ 29).
- Experience the best of classical Sicily by taking in the great Greek temples at Agrigento (➤ 24) or Segesta (➤ 44).
- Visit a vibrant food market and shop for olive oil, pistachio nuts and capers – all Sicilian products.
- Enjoy a taste of one of Italy's chicest resort towns at Taormina (➤ 45).
- Sample some of Sicily's splendid wines, including the unctuous Marsala (➤ 33).
- Bathe in the clear waters that lap Sicily's glorious beaches.
- Explore the interior, a world away from the bustling coast, by driving inland to visit Enna (➤ 31).
- Take in Europe's most active volcano by heading up the slopes of Mount Etna (➤ 35).
- Eat some of the freshest fish you'll ever enjoy at one of the many coastal restaurants, where the fish is straight off the boats.
- Indulge your sweet tooth with fabulous ice cream, a creamy cassata or super-rich cannoli.
- See some of the world's finest Roman mosaics at the Villa Romana near Piazza Armerina (➤ 48).
- Watch the potters at work then browse in a ceramic shop at Sciacca (➤ 51) or Caltagirone (➤ 43).
- Take a drive away from the crowds to walk in the hills and see colourful spreads of springtime wild flowers.

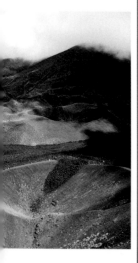

*Breathtaking view over
Mount Etna's summit*

SICILY
how to organise
your time

A Walk in Palermo

This walk leads along main streets and side alleys in central Palermo, with great markets to browse in, flamboyant baroque churches, the city's opera house and plenty of shopping en route.

INFORMATION

Distance 3km (1.8 miles)
Time 2 hours with visits
Start/end point Piazza G Cesare
Lunch Antica Trattoria del Monsù (€–€€)
✉ via Volturno 41
☎ 091 327 774

With your back to the Stazione Centrale, cross Piazza G Cesare and walk straight ahead down via Roma, built in 1922 to connect the old city with via della Libertà. Continue over the crossroads with via Vittorio Emanuele and take the steps down to the right into the Vucciria market (➤ 79).

Follow the market street of via Maccheronai along to your left to emerge on to Piazza San Domenico. Turn left, cross via Roma and walk up via Bandiera to via Maqueda. Cross via Maqueda and walk up via Sant'Agostino, home to the Capo market (➤ 79).

At the top of Sant'Agostino, turn right and walk along, past the Madonna della Mercè, to via Volturno. Turn right and walk towards the monstrously large Teatro Massimo, Palermo's prime opera and ballet venue.

The garden of Villa Giulia is a good place to relax

In front of the Teatro turn right onto via Maqueda, one of the city's most historic streets. Continue to the Quattro Canti, the iconic crossroads of the four old city quarters.

Cross the road to visit the baroque church of San Giuseppe dei Teatini and then continue along via Maqueda. You'll notice the Piazza Pretoria across the road on your left as you walk past the entrance to the Law Faculty of the University. via Maqueda will lead you back to Piazza G Cesare and the station.

A Drive Through the Madonie Mountains

Take this wonderfully varied route into the heart of one of Sicily's most beautiful mountain areas to discover superb scenery and untouched hill towns.

Start in Cefalù (➤ 29) and drive north along the coast towards Messina on the N113. After 8km (4.9 miles) turn right following the signs to Parco Naturale delle Madonie and Castelbuono, a handsome town that spreads itself across the lower slopes of the mountains and bills itself as the capital of the Madonie. Leave town on the N236, following the signs to Geraci Siculo along the road known as the Strada dei Castelli.

Continue deeper and higher into the mountains on the same road for 5.5 (3.4 miles) kilometres to the *bivío* (junction) Geraci. At the junction turn right on the N120, signposted Petralia, and continue for 4.7km (3 miles) to the outskirts of Petralia Soprana. You could pause here – park outside – or continue to Petralia Sottana and fork right, following the signs to Collesano, Piano Battáglia and Piano dei Zucchi. This 15km (9.5-mile) stretch of road climbs through increasingly mountainous country to Piano Battáglia, one of the highest settlements in the Madonie and the centre of a tiny ski area, complete with Swiss-chalet style houses.

Follow the road round to the right at Piano Battáglia, following the signs to Piano dei Zucchi and Isnello. At Piano dei Zucchi continue straight ahead towards Isnello. After 7km (4.3 miles) turn right to Isnello, a very typical inland village. If you want to explore it's a short detour off the main road – follow the signs to the *centro*.

Leave Isnello, and after 2.8km (1.8 miles) turn left and follow the steeply descending road for 22km (13.6 miles) back to Cefalù. This road rejoins the main coastal road on the upper outskirts of Cefalù.

INFORMATION

Distance 135km (84 miles)
Time 7 hours (includes stops)
Start/end point Cefalù
Lunch The Pizzeria da Salvatore (€)
🖂 Piazza San Michele 3, Petralia Soprana
☎ 0921 680169
🕔 Closed Tue; or bring a picnic

A spectacular view over the Madonie en route to Petralia

A Walk in Ortygia, Siracusa

Follow this route to enjoy Siracusa's island heart, where local life ticks over in the shadow of fine classical monuments, medieval palazzi and baroque churches.

Walk across the Ponte Umbertino and through Piazza Pancali to the Tempio di Apollo (6th century BC). Take via Savoia to the right of the temple and walk along to the Porta Marina.

Walk through the gateway and along via Ruggero Settimo until you see trees below you on the right. Turn left up via Collegio. At the T-junction turn right and continue along via Landolina to the Piazza del Duomo (➤ 39).

Walk to the end of the piazza and head straight down via Picharale, bearing right to emerge at the Fonte Aretusa (➤ 39). From here, detour along the lovely, shaded Foro Vittorio Emanuele, known locally as the Marina, a good place to pause. Backtrack to the Fonte and continue on to the Castello Maniace, which dates from 1239, at the end of Ortygia.

Colourful shops and places to eat line Ortygia's historic streets

With your back to the Castello, head down via Salomone, cross the road at the junction and continue along via San Martino. At the junction

with via Capodieci turn right, then almost immediately left down via Roma and continue down the street to Piazza Archimede, Ortygia's main square.

Turn right along via Maestranza and continue to a crossroads and the church of the Immacolata. Turn right here down via Giudecca, then take the second right on to via del Crocifisso. At the junction, turn left, then right to follow via Minerva, which will lead you back to Piazza del Duomo.

A Drive in the Valle d'Anapo

This wonderfully scenic drive heads west from Siracusa to the valley of the River Anapo, visiting baroque Palazzolo Acreide en route.

From Siracusa (➤ 39) take the SR124 through Florídia to Solarino, and then follow the signs to hilltop Palazzolo Acreide (25km/15.6 miles), a beautiful baroque town on a classical site. Stop here for the Casa-Museo Antonino Uccello (via Machiavelli 19, tel 0931 881 499, open daily 9–1, 3:30–7, free), eastern Sicily's finest collection of rural artefacts, and the Akrai, the archaeological remains of an ancient Siracusan city dating from the 7th century BC.

Now take the SR124 (signposted Caltagirone), crossing the River Anapo. At the junction (8km/5 miles) leave the 124, turning right to follow the signs to Ferla, roughly halfway along the route. In Ferla follow the signs to Pantálica, a great Bronze Age necropolis first used between the 10–13th century BC and later the site of classical Hybla. Park at the Castello del Principe entrance (9.5 km/6 miles from Ferla) and follow the path to explore the gorge of the Anapo and the necropolis caves.

Continuing the drive, take the SP10m, with its views to Mount Etna and Catania, to Sortino, home to the Museo Civico dell'Opera dei Pupi (piazza San Francesco 9, tel 0931 952 079, daily 9–1, free), which traces the history of Sicily's traditional puppet theatre.

Follow the signs to Siracusa out of Sortino, looking out for the right turn on to the SP28, which then follows the course of the Anapo. After about 18km (11 miles) the road converges with the SP114. Stay on this to the SR124 exit, which will bring you back into Siracusa to the Parco Archeológico della Neapolis (➤ 40).

INFORMATION

Distance 178km (110 miles)
Time 7 hours (includes stops)
Start/end point Siracusa
Lunch Dell'Arco (€€), via Arco Lantieri, Ferla

The necropolis contains more than 5,000 tombs

17

A Circular Walk in Enna

Follow this route through Enna to take in the heart of the old town and its monuments and enjoy some of Sicily's finest panoramas.

INFORMATION

Distance 3km (1.8 miles)
Time 1.5–2 hours
Start Piazza San Cataldo
End/point Piazza Vittorio Emanuele
Lunch The Bar Azimut (€) near the Castello

With your back to the church of San Cataldo, walk diagonally across Piazza Matteotti and head up via Roma and into Piazza Vittorio Emanuele.

Continue up via Roma, passing San Marco on the left and Piazza Umberto I, another of the string of squares that punctuate via Roma's uphill course, on your right. Walk on up until you see Piazza Colaianni on your right.

Via Roma now leads up past the Duomo (➤ 31) and Piazza Mazzini. Once the street narrows, you're in via Lombardia, which ends in a flourish in a spacious piazza in front of the Castello (➤ 31).

Follow the left-hand road around the castle and past the entrance steps and continue straight on until you can see the rocky mass of the Rocca di Cerere ahead. This is one of Sicily's most ancient holy sites, named after Ceres, the Roman goddess of agriculture, and in the 4th century BC, the site of a magnificent temple.

Magnificent views are waiting to be enjoyed from Enna

Walk back to the front of the Castello and take the right hand street, viale Caterina Savoia, with more views to be glimpsed through the trees, downhill. Follow this down, pass the post office on your right, until you reach Piazza Garibaldi.

Leave the square in the northwest corner and walk down viale Marconi, to the gardens of the belvedere in Piazza Crispi, perhaps Enna's paramount viewpoint, before cutting through and back to Piazza Vittorio Emanuele.

A Drive on Mount Etna's Slopes

There are superb views on this drive, which contours Etna's fertile lower slopes before climbing through lava fields to the Rifugio Sapienza, the jumping off point for tours up the volcano.

Take the A18 autostrada south from Taormina and exit at Fiumefreddo. Follow the signs to Etna Nord on the N120 through pretty Piedimonte Etneo to Linguaglossa, the main tourist centre on Etna's north side (35km/ 21.7 miles).

Continue on the Etna Nord route uphill and through Milo to Zafferano Etnea (21km/ 13 miles), a pleasant hill town, famous for its honey, that attracts hordes of weekend walkers drawn to the trails on the wooded slopes behind the village.

From here, follow the signs to Rifugio Sapienza (19km/11.7 miles), passing through increasingly impressive lava fields.

From Rifugio Sapienza, some 1,400m (4,600 feet) below the summit, a cable car runs further up the mountain, or you can take a guided 4-wheel drive mini-bus tour. This climbs the lava slopes to the Roman Torre del Filósofo, beyond which the southeast active crater of the summit is visible, dramatically spewing smoke; explosions and molten lava are common at this height. You'll traverse lunar landscape to take in the Valle del Bove, a huge chasm almost 20km (32 miles) in circumference and 900m (2,742 feet) deep which comprises almost a sixth of the surface of the volcano. At this height, you'll certainly hear volcanic rumblings and get a whiff of the unforgettable sulphurous smell.

Back in the car, take the Strada dell'Etna, constructed in 1934, downhill to Nicolosi (21km/13 miles), a ski resort that's home to the Museo Vulcanologico Etneo (via Cesare Battisti 32, Fri–Wed 9–1, 4–6; €), which will fill you in on Etna's history and geology.

INFORMATION

Distance 96km (60 miles)
Time Drive 3–4 hours; with volcano visit 6 hours
Start Taormina
End point Nicolosi
Lunch Bar and restaurants at Rifugio Sapienza and towns en route

The smoking crater of active Etna

19

Finding Peace & Quiet

FINDING PEACE AND QUIET

Beautiful, fertile Sicily is a garden, packed with wild delights, superb landscapes and encircled by a magical coastline. If you're looking for tranquillity all you need do is get out of town and into the countryside, while even in summer it's possible to find secluded beaches and quiet, shady corners in busy towns.

WALKING CLOSE TO NATURE

The joys of country walking are little known in Italy, but even in deepest Sicily things are improving, and nowadays you'll find hikes and trails, often way-marked, to suit all tastes. These range from strenuous mountain treks high on the slopes of Etna and through the Nebrodi and Madonie mountains, to strolls through woodlands and down gorges. Botanists too, head for the Madonie, whose limestone flora is among the richest in Italy. In spring, the hills are adrift with flowers, and there's a wide range of orchids and other rare species, many unique to Sicily. You can find these too, on the lower slopes of Etna (► 35) and in the Nebrodi, where the thick woodland encourages a whole different flora. Woodlands too, are good for animals; Sicily has plenty of foxes and wild boar, which you're just as likely to see ambling across a quiet mountain road, complete with a litter of tiny striped piglets. Birders will find delights everywhere, as Sicily's one of the first landfalls north of Africa and an important migratory route, so keep your eyes open for exotics like bee-eaters and the beguiling hoopoe with its butterfly-like flight.

Rural Sicily offers plenty of opportunities to get away from it all

Wild flowers are abundant in spring

THE COAST AND ITS WILDLIFE

Away from the tourist resorts, there are still stretches of empty beaches and quiet coast, where you can bathe and swim in solitude – though be prepared to walk to escape the summer crowds. A top favourite is the Zingaro (► 42), a 7km stretch of unspoilt coast in the far northwest, where tiny coves offer glorious bathing in crystal waters. Good paths run beside the sea and in the hills, and spring brings huge bird numbers and astonishing spreads of brilliant wild flower. Vendicari (► 56), near Siracusa, is another stunner, with superb birdlife on its dunes and wetlands and beautiful sandy beaches for bathing. Other nature reserves, such as the Lago di Lentini and the Saline di Tràpani, are wonderfully peaceful – check out Italy's national parks portal www.parks.it, to find something to suit you.

Sheltered beaches of soft, white sand are ideal for swimming

DO IT ON WHEELS

Cycling as a means of relaxation is virtually unheard of in Sicily, so if you want to tackle the scenic interior from the saddle, you'll have to bring your own wheels – or head for a different type of saddle and join one of the increasing number of pony treks in the main parks; tourist offices will have the relevant details. If strenuous

Head into the interior to discover the real Sicily

exercise fails to appeal, you can still taste the peace and solitude of the great outdoors from the comfort of a car – and see a surprising amount. Just head inland, stop the car, look, listen and smell – wonderful scenery, wind and birdsong, and the scent and vibrant springtime colours of millions of wild-flowers surround you, a true taste of wild Sicily.

What's On

Nearly all traditional festivals have a religious origin and coincide with the great feasts of the church, or local saints' days. All involve parades and processions, music, feasting, drinking and often dancing and fireworks. Throughout the summer, festivals include pilgrimages, fishermen's and harvest festivals, *sagre* (food festivals) devoted to local specialities, and jousting and dancing festivals whose roots lie in the Middle Ages, as do those of Sicily's own dramatic genre, the puppet theatre. Ask at local tourist offices for information, and keep an eye open for posters.

JANUARY	1 New Year's Day
FEBRUARY	Early Feb: Sagra del Mandorlo in Fiore, Agrigento – almond blossom festival with bands, folklore and processions Week before Ash Wednesday: Carnevale at Acireale, Caltanissetta, Trapani, Taormina and Sciacca
APRIL	Holy Week: processions of floats in many towns and villages which reach their climax on Maunday Thursday and Good Friday in Marsala, Caltanissetta, Trapani, Messina and Ragusa
JUNE	Mattanza: tuna fish massacre on Favignana Jun–Jul: ballet festival, Siracusa Jun–Aug: arts festival in Teatro Greco, Taormina
JULY	All month: Estate Musicale Trapanese: outdoor opera at Villa Margherita, Tràpani 2nd week: music festival, Erice 12–15: U Fistinu, spectacular parades and fireworks, Palermo Last week: International Film Festival, Taormina Jul–Aug: Estate Ennese, opera festival, Enna Estate Musicale: music festival in Taormina
AUGUST	All month: Agosto Ibleo, celebrations in Ragusa 13–14: Palio dei Normanni, major medieval jousting festival, Piazza Armerina 13–15: Feast of the Assumption celebrated with procession, music and fireworks all over Sicily
NOVEMBER	1 All Soul's Day
DECEMBER	13 Santa Lucia, processions and fireworks, Siracusa

SICILY's
top 25 sights

The sights are shown on the maps on the inside front cover and inside back cover, numbered **1**–**25** alphabetically

Agrigento

INFORMATION

🔲 B3
Tourist Information Offices
✉ Piazza Vittorio Emanuele
☎ 800 236 837;
   www.agrigento-sicilia.it
🕐 Mon–Fri 8–2, 3–7
🚉 Agrigento

Museo Civico
✉ Santo Spirito, via Foderà
🕐 Mon–Sat 9–1:30
💶 €€
↔ Museo Nazionale
   Archeològico, Agrigento
   (➤ 36); Valley of the
   Temples, Agrigento
   (➤ 47)

Duomo exterior wall

Agrigento, with its medieval core, maze of narrow streets and easy pace of life, is worth visiting before taking in the Greek temples.

The medieval town of Agrigento is a charmer, centred around lively via Atenea, a pretty street lined with shops and cafés, that's the scene of a wonderfully lively *passeggiata* in the evenings. Walk along it from Piazza Aldo Moro to Piazza Sinatra, home to the Municipio (town hall), housed in a 17th-century convent. From here, steep steps and alleys lead to the old upper town, with its whitewashed houses, crumbling *palazzi*, and the church of Santa Maria degli Greci, built on the site of a 5th-century BC Greek temple. Further up, a fine staircase leads to the Duomo, set on a terrace at the highest point of Agrigento. Built in the 14th century, it has a lovely painted ceiling above the nave and some fine baroque tombs.

From here, you could head east downhill to Santo Spirito, an abbey church whose convent buildings house the Museo Civico – the vaulted dormitory with its costume collection is the star turn here. Before you go, ring the bell marked '*monastero*' and buy some of the delectable sweets still made by the nuns, for this convent is one of the few places in Sicily where the old art of confectionery is still in the hands of the people who first worked with sugar. It's also worth strolling along the viale della Vittoria, from where you can look downhill towards the temples and the sea.

Cappella Palatina, Palermo

Deep in the Palazzo dei Normanni, seat of the 12th-century Sicilian kings, the jewel-like Cappella Palatina is Palermo's greatest treasure.

The Cappella Palatina was built between 1132–43 as a private chapel for Roger II. Tolerant in the extreme, Roger commissioned the work from Normans, Greeks and Arabs, ensuring it commemorated the chief religions of Norman Sicily. The ceiling is Arab, the mosaics Greek and Italian, the pulpit and huge paschal candlestick Norman, while Romans laid the intricate pavements. Roger consulted theologians to determine the iconology, most probably to celebrate his monarchy and the power of the Holy Spirit.

The chapel, shimmering with colour and reflected light, is divided by antique columns into a nave and two side aisles, whose floor and lower walls, are paved with white and coloured marble. At the east end is the sanctuary, comprising three apses, each decorated with Byzantine mosaics. The central figure is a wise Christ Pantocrator; on his left, a Madonna and Child, on his right, a Nativity. These are surrounded by New Testament scenes, stories familiar to Roger and his court. The mosaics in the nave, the last to be carried out, show scenes from the Old Testament, including the Creation and the Building of the Ark, while St Peter and Paul appear in the scenes in the aisles. The dais at the back of the nave was Roger's vantage point for services. Don't miss examining the Easter candlestick, carved with more than a hundred intricate animal forms.

INFORMATION

* B1
* Piazza Indipendenza
* 091 705 7003/ 091 705 4096; www.federicosecondo.org
* Mon–Sat 8:30–12, 2–5; Sun 8:30–12
* Restaurants in piazza outside
* Linea A + 104, 105, 108, 304, 309
* None
* €€€
* Cattedrale (► 28); Catacombe dei Cappuccini (► 26), Galleria Regionale Siciliane (► 52); Museo Archeológico (► 52); Museo delle Marionette (► 52); San Cataldo (► 54); La Martorana (► 54); San Francesco d'Assisi (► 54), all in Palermo

Detailed carving of a lion

Catacombe dei Cappuccini, Palermo

INFORMATION

- ✚ B1
- ✉ via Cappuccini 1
- ☎ 091 212 117
- 🕐 9–12, 3–5:30
- 🍴 Bars nearby on via Cappuccini
- 🚌 327
- ♿ None
- 💷 Free but leave donation
- ↔ Cappella Palatina (➤ 25); Cattedrale (➤ 28); Galleria Regionale Siciliane (➤ 52); Museo Archeológico (➤ 52); Museo delle Marionette (➤ 52); San Cataldo (➤ 54); La Martorana (➤ 54); San Francesco d' Assisi (➤ 54), all in Palermo

This macabre underground cemetery in west Palermo, containing over 8,000 mummified corpses, has been luring visitors since the 16th century.

The Capuchin monks have a long tradition of preserving and displaying the remains of their dead, either as tableaux of bones artistically arranged, or by embalming the body. In the 16th century they used the catacombs beneath their church on the outskirts of Palermo to do just this, and it wasn't long before lay people were clamouring for the same process. You can see the result today – over 8,000 bodies dating from the 16th to the early years of the 20th centuries.

Bodies were preserved by a variety of chemical and drying processes, some of which took up to eight months, and then, dressed in clothes chosen before death, allocated a niche or wall space in the underground corridors. Like were grouped with like – soldiers here, lawyers there, virgins and spinsters in their own area. The sight is macabre in the extreme, but there's poignancy too, in the sheer numbers of babies and young children who died in infancy. The most recent and saddest of all is 2-year-old Rosalia Lombardo, perfectly preserved by a secret embalming process in 1920 the method of which has already been lost.

Embalmed bodies line the walls of Palermo's macabre visitor attraction

Catacombe di San Giovanni, Siracusa

Beneath the ruined church of San Giovanni, you can explore the huge catacombs used by Siracusa's early Christians to bury their dead.

Banned from burying church members within the city, early Christians were forced to look elsewhere and took over the tunnels that had once acted as the Greek water supply. The system was huge, a series of reservoirs linked by passages which today form a series of catacombs second only in size to those of Rome. This underground world is reached beneath the ruins of the church of San Giovanni, a Norman church built on the site of Siracusa's earliest cathedral. It was destroyed in the earthquake of 1693, but the crypt, supposedly the site of St Paul's mission to the Siracusans and scene of the martyrdom of St Marcian, first bishop of the city, is intact and gives access to the catacombs.

The guided tour takes you through this astounding underground world, used from Roman times through to the 6th century. The walls are honeycombed with niches, used as burial places, though the bodies have been removed and buried elsewhere. Look out for the traces of early Christian paintings on the walls, and the incised symbols of Christianity – a fish, a lamb and a cross. It's an eerie place that gives an insight into the difficulties of the early church as it took on the power of the pagan world.

INFORMATION

- ✚ D3
- ✉ via San Giovanni alla Catacombe
- ☎ 0931 64694
- ◷ 9:30–12:30, 2:30–4:30
- 🍴 Bars and restaurants nearby
- ♿ None
- 💶 €€
- ↔ Archaeological zone, Siracusa (► 40); Ortygia, Siracusa (► 39); Museo Archeológico Paolo Orsi (► 53); Duomo, Siracusa (► 54)

Ruined façade of San Giovanni church

Cattedrale, Palermo

The golden bulk of Palermo's Cattedrale, among the largest Norman survivors, rises to one side of the arrow-straight via Vittorio Emanuele.

Founded in 1185 and built on the site of an earlier Byzantine structure, Palermo's cathedral was the brainchild of an Englishman, Walter of the Mill, who was Archbishop of Palermo and tutor to the young William II. The apses and towers at the east end of the exterior are the best Norman relics, mirrored by two towers at the west end. The main entrance is a superb Catalan-Gothic three-arched porch, finally finished in 1426. The stonework round the door shows Norman work, the serene Virgin above is older still and the left hand column has an Arabic inscription from the Koran, a survivor of the mosque which once stood here.

The interior was altered in the 18th-century, when the decoration was removed and the high altar dismantled – statues from it are scattered round the church. On the right, you'll find the entrance to the Treasury, containing the Norman crown (1210) of Constance of Aragon and the crypt, burial place of Archbishop Walter.

At the back of the church are six royal tombs, the final resting places of the Norman dynasty. Here lie buried Roger II (died 1154) and his daughter Constance (died 1198), Constance's husband, the Emperor Henry VI Hohenstaufen (died 1197) and their son, Frederick II (died 1250), a king so powerful he was known as Stupor Mundi, the marvel of the world.

The cathedral's imposing main entrance

Duomo, Cefalù

The lovely coastal town of Cefalù, with its medieval centre, is home to a magnificent Duomo, among the finest of Sicily's Norman churches.

Tight against the soaring crag of La Rocca rise the towers of Roger II's cathedral, started in 1131, unfinished at his death in 1154 and consecrated in 1267. Steps lead from a piazza to the arched entrance and the cool, dark interior of one of Sicily's most perfect Norman churches. It stands on a Roman site and the nave is lined with 16 Roman columns, taken from an ancient Temple of Diana, and roofed with a 13th-century ceiling. The apse contains a glittering Christ Pantocrator, the Virgin, angels and saints, all set against a gold background. These are the earliest and best-preserved Norman mosaics in Sicily, executed by Greek craftsmen and completed in 1148.

The streets of old Cefalù surround the Duomo, with via Ruggiero, the main drag, running straight down towards the old harbour and its fishing boats. Off this branch narrow lanes; one is home to the Museo Mandralisca. East from the old town, beautiful beaches stretch out, attracting summer-time masses – you can escape the hordes by climbing the Rocca and enjoying some of the best views on the north coast.

INFORMATION

✚ C2
Duomo
✉ Piazza del Duomo
🕐 Apr–Sep daily 8–2, 3:30–8; Oct–Mar 8–12, 3:30–7
🍴 Bars and restaurants in Piazza del Duomo
♿ Poor via steps; ask inside for help
💶 Free
❓ Occasional concerts, details from tourist office

Tourist Information Office
✉ Corso Ruggero 77
☎ 0921 421 050 www.cefalu-tour.pa.it; www.cefaluinforma.it
🕐 Apr–Sep Mon–Sat 9–8, Sun 9–1; Oct–Mar Mon–Sat 8–2, 3–7
🚉 Cefalù

Museo Mandralisca
✉ via Mandralisca 13
☎ 0921 421 541; www.museomandralisca.it
🕐 Easter–Sep daily 9–7; Oct–Easter daily 9–noon
🍴 Bars and restaurants nearby
♿ Good if lift is working
💶 €€

Cafés in Piazza Duomo are ideal for relaxing after exploring the old town

Duomo, Monreale

This Norman cathedral, set in the hills of southwest Palermo, has superb mosaics, a pageant of Byzantine images that tell the Christian story.

INFORMATION

- B1/B2
- Piazza Duomo
- 091 640 4413
- Daily 8–6. Treasury daily 8:30–12:30, 3:30–6
- Bars and restaurants in Piazza del Duomo
- 389 from Palermo (Piazza Indipendenza)
- Good
- Duomo free, treasury and terrace €€, cloister €€€
- Palermo
- Occasional concerts

Monreale cathedral was built by William II in 1174 as a counter-balance to Archbishop Walter's power in Palermo. No expense was spared, and the result is the artistically greatest of all the Norman religious foundations. You can admire the exterior, with its magnificent apses and arches, before entering through the great bronze doors to be overwhelmed by the sheer scale of the interior mosaics, the world's second-largest mosaic-covered surface.

The mosaics tell the story of the Old and New Testaments, a medieval strip cartoon with scenes such as the Creation, Adam and Eve expelled from Paradise, the animals entering Noah's Ark, Abraham's sacrifice, and, in the transepts, the whole story of the life of Jesus, from the Annunciation of his birth to his death on the Cross. The huge figures in the apse were the work of Byzantine Greek masters and show Christ Pantocrator looming in benediction over the Virgin and ranks of the saint. Don't miss the exquisite marble and mosaic dado beneath the mosaics, and you might want to see the opulent reliquaries in the treasury before climbing the 180 steps to the terrace – an effort rewarded with superb views to Palermo and the sea.

To the right of the cathedral is the 12-century Benedictine cloister. The 228 twin columns, the work of French masters from Burgundy, are each different, the capitals showing scenes from everyday life, animals, birds and foliage, biblical scenes, monsters and classical themes.

Christ Pantocrator watches over his flock in glorious mosaic form

Enna

Perched high in the very centre of Sicily, Enna is the epitome of a fortress town, a stony and secretive place with breathtakingly wide views.

Known as 'the navel of Sicily', Enna stands 935m (2,844 feet) above sea level, a strategic citadel that was fought over by Greeks, Romans, Arabs and Normans. The main reminder of this past is the 13th-century Castello (open daily 9–1, 3–5; free), built by Frederick II high on the easternmost spur of Enna's craggy ridge. It's a massive fortress, the three inner keeps ringed with thick walls and the six towers that remain of the original 20. One of them, the Torre Pisano, can be climbed and will reward you with views that take in vast sweeps of the countryside, with Etna's slopes prominent to the east.

From the Castello via Roma runs down the ridge through a series of squares to Piazza Vittorio Emanuele, a lovely square that's the hub of Enna's nightly passeggiata. Roughly halfway down via Roma, you'll find the Duomo, built in 1307. Damaged and restored over the years, its interior is a treat, an exuberantly decorated space where the apricot walls and white stucco contrast with the massively carved columns. Head on down to Piazza Garibaldi, dominated by some monumental Fascist public buildings, and walk through to Piazza Crispi, which has a wonderful belvedere, from where you'll look across to the Arab-founded village of Calascibetta, its ochre houses tumbling down the hill, and over the dreamy landscape.

INFORMATION

⊞ C2/C3
Tourist Information Office
✉ via Roma 413
☎ 0935 528 228;
   www.apt-enna.com
🕐 Mon–Sat 9–1, 3:30–6:30
🚩 Enna
↔ Villa Romana del Casale,
   Piazza Armerina (➤ 48)

Detail of one of the magnificent paintings in the Duomo

Erice

Erice, one of Sicily's most beautiful, picturesque villages, is perched high above the western coast with superb views to Trapani and the sea.

Castello di Venere

Founded more than 3,000 years ago as a shrine to Venus, Erice is shaped like an equilateral triangle, with the main entrance, Porta Trapani, set at the southwest angle. From here, it's just a few yards to the cathedral church, the Matrice (May–Sep daily 10–7, Oct–Apr daily 10:30–12:30), whose wonderful fortified Gothic façade belies the 19th-century interior. To one side rises a detached campanile, built by Frederick III around 1315 as a lookout tower. From here, via Vittorio Emanuele runs up towards Piazza Umberto I, the only large open space in town. As you climb, you'll get glimpses into the flower-filled hidden courtyards of the stony houses, and walk past shops selling Erice's famous *pasticcerie*. The Piazza is home to the Museo Comunale Cordici (Mon–Sat 8:30–12:30, 3–5), housed in a long 19th-century neoclassical building. The diverse collection includes a beautiful Head of Aphrodite, dating from the 5th century BC, and a superb marble Annunciation by Antonello Gagini.

From here, your best sightseeing bet is simply to wander at will, exploring the myriad *vanelle*, alleys, peeping into courtyards and tiny *piazze*, scrambling up and down cobbled steps and popping into whichever of the town's numerous churches happens to be open. Eventually you should find yourself at the Castello di Venere, site of the classical shrine.

Marsala

Lovely and historic Marsala, the westernmost town in Sicily, is best known for its production of Marsala, a fortified sweet dessert wine.

Ancient Marsala was home to Greeks, Carthaginians and Romans, an important and rich city, trading with Africa. From here, Scipio Africanus finally conquered Carthage, and later, the Arabs named the town Marsah-al-Allah, the 'port of God'. Still prosperous in the Middle Ages, it really came into its own in 1773, when the Englishman John Woodhouse started the wine trade, and in 1860 Garibaldi landed here, making it the first city of a united Italy.

It's a fine town sprinkled with trees and greenery, its historic core approached through gates in the surrounding walls. To the west, a broad expanse of wasteland, once the heart of the Roman city and scattered with archaeological excavations, stretches to the sea. On the seafront you'll find the Museo Archeologico, which displays finds from Marsala's past, including the remains of a Phoenician galley, found in the 1980s on the seabed off the island of Mòzia (➤ 37). Heading east, walk through the Porta Garibaldi to Piazza della Repubblica, the main square that's home to the cathedral; near here, the Museo degli Arazzi displays a set of eight fine 16th-century Flemish tapestries, a gift to the city. Sightseeing over, head for one of the Marsala companies, to learn more about the wine trade and taste some of the wines.

Fine local produce

INFORMATION

➕ A2
Tourist Information Office
✉ via XI Maggio 100
☎ 0923 714 097/993 270; www.lagunablu.org
🕐 Mon–Sat 8–8, Sun 9–12
🍴 Bars and restaurants in town
🚌 Marsala

Museo Archeológico
✉ via Lungomare Boeo
🕐 Mon–Fri & Sat 9–1, Wed & Sat 9–1, 4–7
♿ Good
💰 €€

Wine Tasting
Stabilimento Florio
✉ Lungomare Mediterraneao
☎ 0923 723 846
🕐 Guided visits Mon–Fri 10–11, 3:30–4:30, Sat 9:30–10:30, 11–12
♿ Fair
🔄 Trapani (➤ 51); Museo Whitaker, Mòzia (➤ 37); Mazara del Vallo (➤ 34)

Mazara del Vallo

Bustling Mazara combines its role as one of Italy's main fishing ports with that of an animated and attractive town, one of the liveliest in western Sicily.

Historically the most important of Sicily's Moorish towns, Mazara del Vallo makes the most of its seafront position, with a shady lungomare and gardens stretching along the waterfront to the fishing port, home to one of Italy's biggest fishing fleets. It's this combination of hard-working, earthy port and the splendid baroque churches and civic buildings of the old centre that gives the town its charm, and there's nowhere in western Sicily with a stronger north African atmosphere.

Head for the Tunisian quarter, or Casbah, home to many of the north Africans that work the boats, and wander the maze of souk-like streets – mainstream Sicily seems far away. Southeast of here, the beautiful Piazza della Repubblica is home to the Duomo, flanked by a mix of baroque buildings, complete with porticoes and arcades. Near here, the Museo del Satiro displays a bronze Dancing Satyr more than 2.4m (8 feet) high, the torso was caught by local fishermen in the waters near the island of Pantelleria in 1998. A few weeks later the left leg was found, and hope remains that one day the arms and other leg will rise from the deep in the nets.

The nave of the Duomo

Mount Etna

Trailing its signature plume of smoke, the brooding presence of Mount Etna, the smouldering giant that's Europe's most active volcano, dominates eastern Sicily.

Dazzling in the sun, Mount Etna (3,323m/10,902 feet) at other times, with clouds wreathing its summit, appears sinister and menacing, a constant reminder of the appalling powers of death and destruction it holds. From the upper slopes, where lava fields trace the routes of past eruptions, views across the whole island and into Calabria open up, while its lower slopes are fertile beyond measure, planted with vines and olives.

This is the highest volcano in Europe and among the world's most active. The ancients called it Aetna and believed it was the site of Vulcan's forge, and throughout the centuries its eruptions have engulfed farmland, towns and Catania itself, with lava flows reaching as far as the sea. Today, vulcanologists agree that the main crater is becoming increasingly active. In July 2001 a series of complex explosions started on the southeast side, opening up 18 temporary craters, which poured out fountains of fiery lava. In 2002 an earthquake triggered activity on both the north and south flanks, threatening the towns of Nicolosi and Linguaglossa and destroying the ski resort of Piano Provenzano. Bulldozers were used to build dykes and divert the flow and the damage was contained, but further eruptions were inevitable, and occurred in 2004. The whole area is a regional park, with a unique geology, flora and fauna, and its traditional farming and way of life are protected.

INFORMATION

🔲 D2
Etna Tourist Information Offices
Randazzo
✉ via Umberto I 197
☎ 095 799 1611;
   www.prg.it/parcodelletna
   (Italian only)
🕐 Daily 9–1, 3–7
🍴 Restaurants and bars
   in town
🚃 Randazzo, Circumetnea
   Line

Nicolosi
✉ via Etnea 107/A
☎ 959 14588;
   www.prg.it/parcodelletna
   (Italian only)
🕐 Mon–Fri 9–2, 4:30–7
🍴 Restaurants and bars
   in town
🔁 Taormina (➤ 46)
   Catania (➤ 50)

Walkers approaching the crater's rim

Museo Nazionale Archeológico, Agrigento

INFORMATION

➕ B3
The Museo Nazionale Archeológico
✉ via dei Templi, Contrada San Nicola
☎ 0922 401 565
🕐 Tue–Sat–7, Mon & Sun 9–1
🍴 Snack bar in museum €
♿ Fair
🎫 €€€
↔ Agrigento (➤ 24)
Valley of the Temples, Agrigento (➤ 47)

One of the giant figures from the Temple of Zeus

The statues, artefacts and superb Greek vases in this wonderful museum help clothe the bare bones of history shown in Agrigento's excavations.

To add another dimension to your visit to the Valle dei Templi head for the outstanding Archeological Museum, which contains finds from the temples and ancient city, as well as the surrounding area. It's a very fine collection, strong both historically and aesthetically, and many of the exhibits will help bring ancient Akragas alive. You'll want to concentrate on the 11 rooms of the first section, which display finds from Agrigento and its territory, and represent the full flowering of the great Hellenistic civilisations. There are superb marble figures and red and black vases from the 5th–3rd centuries BC, marble statues and busts of Persephone and the goddess Aphrodite, coins, inscriptions and votive figures. Don't miss the vases in room 3, which date from the 3rd century BC and include a 440 BC whiteground krater depicting Perseus freeing Andromeda. Room 6 has finds from the Temple of Zeus, including a reconstructed telamon from its façade, while room 10 has a marble statue of Ephebus (5th century BC) an athletic young man, thought to represent a participant at the Olympic Games.

If you've got time, you can walk across the road from the museum to take in the Hellenistic-Roman quarter, an excavated residential area of the city, its houses still retaining their mosaic floors.

Museo Whitaker, Mòzia

A tiny island in a lagoon is the site of the 8th century BC Phoenician city of Mòzia and home to a wonderful archaeological museum.

Take a boat to land on this island, where you can follow winding footpaths to discover the fascinating, if scanty, excavations of what, 3,000 years ago, was one of Sicily's most powerful cities, first excavated by Pip Whitaker (1850–1936), the Englishman who owned the island in the 19th century. The museum is housed in the villa he built, and contains the collection he amassed, either on site, or by purchase from dealers. There are over 1,000 stelae, grave markers, as well as huge amounts of pottery, masks and divine images, all in terracotta – look out for the smiling image mask of the god Bes. Other cases contain the jewellery and glassware so loved by the Phoenicians, pendants and collars in gold and bronze and tiny braziers used for burning aromatics as perfume.

These treasures, though, are all put in the shade by the main draw, the so-called Charioteer. Discovered in 1979, this example of the finest of Greek sculpture is thought to be the work of the master Pheidias, c440 BC. It shows a self-confident young man, his muscles rippling beneath the his tunic. Sculpted in white marble, it's a stunning work, a piece of such cold beauty it still has the power to move us today.

INFORMATION

- A2
- Mòzia
- 0923 712 598
- Apr–Oct 9–12.45, 3–6; Nov–Mar 9–3, may be subject to change
- Restaurant and bar on island (summer only) (€€)
- Mozia Line, tel 360 356 053, www.mozialine.com; Apr–Oct 9–12.45, 3–6; Nov–Mar 9–3. Follow brown signs to Isole Stagnone from village of San Leonardo
- AST buses run from Piazza del Popolo in Marsala to the ferry (Mon–Sat 8–6, every 60–90 minutes, journey time 30 minutes)
- Access poor (boat); site poor, museum good
- €€€
- Trapani (➤ 51) Marsala (➤ 33)

The ferry that serves the island

Noto

INFORMATION

🔁 D4

Tourist Information Office

✉ Piazzale XVI Maggio, C0931 896 654/0931 573779

🕐 Mon–Fri 9–2, 3:30–6:30, Sat 9–12, 3:30–6:30

🕐 Museums and churches open 9–1, 3:30–7

🍴 Restaurant and cafés along Corso Vittorio Emanuele

🚻 Noto

♿ Good along Corso Vittorio Emanuele; poor elsewhere

❓ The town centre is floodlit in the evenings

🔁 Ragusa (▶ 41)

Ornate fountain outside San Domenico church

The honey-coloured stone of the harmonious streets and sublime buildings of Noto make it the loveliest of all Sicily's baroque towns.

Built after the 1693 earthquake to replace an older town, Noto is the work of the finest architects of the age, whose brief was to co-operate in the design of a city that synthesised all that was most innovative – wide streets, squares to act as focal points, vistas and stairways to lead the eye from one area to the next.

The main street, the majestic Corso Vittorio Emmanuele, runs along the flank of a hill from the Porta Reale, and passes many of the town's main monuments. The first of these are the churches of Santa Chiara and San Francesco and San Salvatore monastery, followed by the Piazza Municipio, where church and state, in the shape of two of the town's most compelling buildings, the cathedral of San Nicolo and the serene neoclassical Palazzo Ducezio (1746), Noto's town hall, face each other across a piazza. Next to the cathedral is the Palazzo Vescovile (Bishop's Palace) and the Palazzo Sant'Alfano Landolina, while beyond is the basilica of San Salvatore and the church of the Collegio, its audacious curved façade the perfect fanfare to its frothy white and gilded stucco interior. Then comes Piazzale XVI Maggio, home to the charming Teatro Civico and the soaring convex façade of San Domenico church (1737–56). Elsewhere, you can marvel open-mouthed at the Palazzo Villadorata, a perfect example of the mind-blowing opulence of the 18th-century nobility's taste.

Ortygia, Siracusa

The tiny island of Ortygia, site of the original 8th-century BC city, is crammed with remnants of the past in the shape of ruins, churches and palaces.

Ortygia, 1km (0.5 mile) in length and barely 500m (450 yards) across, is connected to the mainland by two bridges. Walk across the Ponte Umbertino to see the ruins of the Doric Tempio di Apollo (Temple of Apollo), built in the early 6th century BC. From here, Corso Matteoti runs up to the main square, Piazza Archimede. Near here is the beautiful Piazza del Duomo, an elongated space surrounded by harmonious 17th- and 18th-century buildings. On one side stands the Duomo (► 54), built where the goddess Athena's shrine once stood and incorporating the Doric columns of the 5th-century BC pagan temple – no other building in Sicily illustrates the island's layers of civilisation better. The temple, one of the richest in the ancient world, was converted into a Christian church and became the cathedral in 640. Its superbly ebullient façade was added after the 1693 earthquake, and contrasts with the shadowy and muted interior, more pagan than Christian in atmosphere.

Through the piazza, another street leads down to the Fonte Aretusa, the freshwater spring that attracted the first settlers. From here you can see Frederick II's Castello Maniace, built in 1239, to the south, walk along the tree-lined waterfront or head for the Museo Regionale, whose chief treasures are a serene Annunciation by Antonello da Messina and Caravaggio's wonderful Burial of St Lucy.

INFORMATION

➕ D3
Tourist Information Office
✉ via della Maestranza 33 (Ortygia)
☎ 0931 464 255; www.apt-siracusa.it
🕐 Mon–Fri 8–2 and 2:30–5:30, Sat 8–2

Duomo
✉ Piazza del Duomo
☎ 0931 65328
🕐 7:30–6 except during services
♿ Fair

Museo Regionale d'Arte Medioevale e Moderna
✉ via Capodieci 14
☎ 0931 69511
🕐 Tue–Sat 9–1:30, Sun 9–12:30
♿ Poor
💶 €€
🔗 Archaeological zone, (► 40); Catacombs, (► 27); Duomo (► 54), all Siracusa

A relaxing way to see the sights

Parco Archeológico della Neapolis

INFORMATION

➕ D3
Parco Archeológico
della Neapolis
✉ viale Teocrito
☎ 0931 65068
🕐 Daily 9–7
🍴 Snack bar on site €
♿ Good surfaces
　throughout site but no
　access to Teatro Greco
💶 €€€
❓ Summer classical theatre
　at Teatro Greco
↔ Catacombs, Siracusa
　(➤ 27); Ortygia, Siracusa
　(➤ 39); Museo
　Archeológico Paolo Orsi
　(➤ 53); Duomo, Siracusa
　(➤ 54)

Cavernous entrance to
Orecchio di Dionisio

Vast and romantic quarries, worked in ancient times, a superb museum and a Greek theatre make visiting Siracusa's archeological zone an unforgettable experience.

Siracusa's northern boundaries have been marked for over 2,000 years by the latomie, a string of quarries, whose stone – an estimated 5 billion cubic metres – was used to build the classical city. This ancient and sophisticated civilisation is the focus of the Museo Archeológico Paolo Orsi (➤ 53), a serious and scholarly museum tracing the history of both the pre-Greeks and Greeks in Sicily.

Nearby is the Neapolis, a sprawling archeological park centred around the latomie themselves. Near the entrance is the Ara di Ierone II, a 3rd-century BC altar, which you'll pass en route to the Latomia del Paradiso, the largest quarry of all, the 3rd-century Anfiteatro Romano, and the Teatro Greco.

This is indubitably the star turn, a wonderfully preserved theatre, first constructed in the 5th century BC, and adapted by the Romans for gladiatorial combat. Forty-two of its 59 rows of seats still surround the stage, from where the acoustics enable every word to be heard right to the highest tier, making it a wonderful venue for Siracusa's summer arts festival of performances of Greek plays. Follow the path from here to the Latomie, where you can wander along paths lined with orange and almond trees to reach the Orecchio di Dionisio (Dionysius' Ear), a huge cavernous quarry whose name was the inspiration of the painter Caravaggio, impressed by its acoustic properties.

Ragusa

The twin towns of Ragusa and Ragusa Ibla, tumbling down a hilly ridge, are a happy mix of medieval stepped streets, tiny lanes, 18th-century squares and splendid baroque buildings.

Ragusa Superiore, the upper town, was built after the 1693 earthquake, and laid out on a perfect grid pattern. Its main street is the Corso Italia, arrowing down the hill towards the old town, and scattered with some monumental palazzi. Here you'll find the Cattedrale, while nearby is the Museo Archeológico.

Ragusa Ibla, the lower town, retains its medieval layout, the combination of huddled alleys with splendid monuments and spacious squares giving it a unique charm. It's approached via steps leading past the restored 15th-century church of Santa Maria della Scala. From here, narrow alleys will bring you to the heart of Ibla, the beautiful, irregular and theatrical Piazza del Duomo, adorned with stately palms, that slopes down from the Duomo di San Giorgio, designed by Rosario Gagliardi and considered one of the masterpieces of Sicilian baroque. Its three-tiered façade, approached through stupendous iron gates up a flight of graceful steps, is further dramatised by its position, set at an angle to the piazza. Walk through the square to stunning Piazza Pola, containing another Gagliardi church, San Giuseppe. Beyond here lies the Giardino Ibleo, a well-planted and shady park, which contains three more churches and is approached from the portal of the 15th-century Gothic San Giorgio Vecchio, the only remnant of a vast pre-earthquake church, and the symbol of Ragusa Ibla.

INFORMATION

➕ C4
Tourist Information Office
✉️ Piazza San Giovanni, Ragusa Superiore
☎️ 0923 676 635; www.comune.ragusa.it
🕐 Mon–Sat 9–1 & 4–7, Sun 10–12

Museo Archeológico
✉️ via Natalelli,
☎️ 0923 622 963
🕐 Tue–Sun 9–1:30, 4–7:30
💶 €€
♿ Good

Duomo
✉️ Piazza del Duomo
🕐 Daily 9–12:30 & 4–7
♿ Fair
🔄 Noto

San Giacomo church in Giardino Ibleo

Riserva Naturale dello Zingaro

INFORMATION

🔢 A1

🍴 Bars and restaurants in Castellammare del Golfo and Torre dell'Impiso

🅿 Castellammare del Golfo

♿ Access into the park is on foot only

🔄 Castellammare del Golfo (► 50); San Vito lo Capo (► 55)

Park Office

✉ via Segesta 197, Castellammare del Golfo

☎ 0924 35108; www.riservazingaro.it

An unspoilt stretch of magnificent coastline, backed by hills rich in rare wild flowers and home to varied birds and animals.

Established in 1981, the Zingaro nature reserve was set up after local protests at a government plan to drive a road along the coast in an effort to curtail Mafia use of the hidden coves as drug-smuggling bases. There are still no roads, and entrance from the east is via the old tuna fishing village of Scopello, site of the park information office, where you can pick up maps, and from the northwest via San Vito lo Capo (► 55).

The reserve covers 1,650ha (4,075 acres) and stretches for 7km (4 miles) along a beautiful coastline, where steep slopes plunge to a succession of idyllic coves, tiny bays and clear water. The main track follows the coast and you can walk along to the succession of lovely coves – Capreria, Marinella and Uzzo are 1, 3 and 7km (1, 2, 4 miles) along the path, and offer superb bathing and snorkelling.

Other paths fan out through the hills, with Monte Speziale (913m/ 2,290 feet) the highest point. The inland landscape is varied, and there are shelters and three separate museums that fill in the story of the area. Most visitors head for the hills in the spring, when the wonderful flora is at its

Colourful resident of the nature reserve

best and there's the chance to see rare raptors and other birds. If you're walking any distance take food and water with you, there are no supplies within the reserve.

Scala di Santa Maria del Monte, Caltagirone

This magnificent flight of stairs, decorated from top to bottom with colourful tiles, dominates the centre of Caltagirone, a city built of golden sandstone.

High in the hills behind the southeast coast, stands Caltagirone, 'Queen of the Hills'. It's a beautiful city, its churches, palaces and civic buildings lavishly decorated with the colourful ceramic tiles for which it's famed. Via Roma runs into the historic centre, passing over the Ponte San Francesco, an 18th-century viaduct brilliant with majolica decoration. This leads into Piazza Umberto and the adjacent Piazza del Municipio, which frames Caltagirone's most astounding monument, the Scala Santa Maria del Monte.

This flight of 142 steep stairs leads up to the baroque church of the same name; each step is tiled in white, yellow, blue and green, and every tile is different. Climb up to the top and you'll pass tiny ceramic workshops and be rewarded with fine views over the town. The steps were built in the 17th century to link the church at the top with the Cathedral; a road had been planned, but the incline was too steep. They were originally plain, the tiles being added in 1954. The stairs look their most magical on July 24th and 25th each year, when they are illuminated with coloured paper lanterns in honour of San Giacomo, St James.

INFORMATION

➕ C3
Tourist Information Office
✉ via Volta Libertini 3
☎ 0933 53809;
   www.comune.
   caltagirone.ct.it
🕐 Mon–Fri 9–1, 4–7, Sat 9–1

🍽 Restaurants and bars in
   Caltagirone
🚏 Caltagirone
♿ Poor, but stairs visible
   from below

Each step of this staircase is decorated with hand-painted tiles

Segesta

INFORMATION

➕ A2

✉️ Segesta

☎️ 0924 952 356

🕐 Daily 9–7 (ticket office closes at 6)

🍴 Snack bar in museum shop €

🚌 Buses from Piazza Malta in Tràpani Mon–Sat 8, 10, 2 and 5, returning 1:10, 4:10 and 6:30

♿ Poor

💶 €€€

❓ Occasional performances of Greek plays; summer shuttle bus runs from ticket office up to theatre

↔️ Castellammare del Golfo

This magnificent hilltop Doric temple and its nearby theatre, standing in isolated country, is Sicily's most compelling and evocative classical site.

Egesta, modern Segesta, was the principle city of the Elymians, legendary survivors of the Trojan war, who settled on the slopes of Monte Barbaro in the 12th century BC. By the 5th century BC they were thoroughly Hellenised, and the temple, dating between 426 and 416 BC is certainly the work of a great Athenian architect. As you stand below, this beautiful golden masterpiece looks complete, its 36 columns, entablature and pediment enclosing a space minus a roof. Climb up though, and you'll see how unfinished the building is – the columns lack the typical Doric fluting, the *cella* and roof were never built and the stone bosses on the stairs, used to manhandle the stone on to the site, still remain in place.

Segesta's white theatre lies across from the temple, high on a hill with views across the slopes and plains to the sea. It was bang in the centre of the city and is surrounded by excavations that have thrown some light onto Segesta's past. Built around or before the 3rd century BC, it is one of the best-preserved of all classical theatres, with a diameter of 63m (205 feet) and its 20 rows of seats, facing north to the distant sea, capable of accommodating 3,200 spectators.

On a rocky outcrop stands the amazing but unfinished temple at Segesta

Taormina

Set in a superb position above the shining blue sea, Taormina is Sicily's best-known resort, an idyllic town that attracts virtually every visitor to the island.

From the Teatro Greco (▶ 46), head through shady Piazza Vittorio Emanuele for the Corso Umberto, Taormina's main street, which runs the length of the town. It's lined with 14th- and 15th-century palazzi, now housing tempting shops, and, halfway along, widens out into Piazza IX Aprile, a beautiful open space that contains the churches of Sant'Agostino and San Giuseppe and offers superlative views and inviting cafés. Walk through the restored, 12th-century Torre dell'Orologio (clocktower), to continue down the oldest part of the street to the 13th-century Duomo, a low-key charmer fronted by a pretty fountain. From here you can back-track through the alleys and stepped streets that surround the Corso – take your time, there's something of delight to be found around every flower-dripping corner, including the Naumachia, an entire, late-Roman wall.

The 19th-century Brits loved Taormina, and it was a 19th-century British gentlewoman, Florence Trevelyan, who, in 1899, created Taormina's lovely public gardens, signposted everywhere as the Villa Comunale. Forced to leave Britain in a hurry after an affair with the future Edward VII, she took solace in creating one of Sicily's loveliest green spaces on a terrace above the sea, an enchanting green oasis that's packed with exotic year-round interest. There are views from here down to the sea, and beach-lovers can take the cable car down to Taormina's pretty coast – a beguiling mix of rocky coves, caves and sandy beaches.

INFORMATION

➕ D2

Tourist Information Office

✉ Palazzo Corvaja, Piazza Vittorio Emmanuele

☎ 0942 23243; www.gate2taormina.com

🕐 Mon–Sat 8:30–2, 4–7

Villa Comunale

✉ via Bagnoli Croce

🕐 Daily 8–8

♿ Fair

Cable Car

✉ via Pirandello

☎ 0942 23906

🕐 Jun–Aug daily 8:30–2am; Sep–May daily 8:30–8:15

💶 €€

🔁 Teatro Greco, Taormina (▶ 46); Giardini-Naxos (▶ 55), Mount Etna (▶ 35)

Gardens at Villa Comunale

Teatro Greco, Taormina

INFORMATION

- D2
- via Teatro Greco
- 0942 23220
- Dec–Feb daily 9–4:30; 1–15 Mar & Nov daily 9–5; 16–31 Mar & mid- to end Oct daily 9–5:30; Apr, Sep to mid-Oct daily 9–6:30; May–Aug daily 9–7
- Restaurants and bars in Taormina
- Taormina
- Poor
- €€€
- Venue for summer arts festival (➤ 22)
- Taormina (➤ 45); Giardini-Naxos (➤ 55), Mount Etna (➤ 35)

One of the most perfectly sited of all Greek theatres stands high above the sea in Taormina, with snow-capped Mount Etna rising to the south.

It's hard to imagine a more perfect backdrop for a theatre than here, where the audience can drink in views of the sea, the coasts of Calabria and Sicily and the snow-capped slopes of Etna, a vista that surely puts paid to the theory that the Greeks built their theatres wherever it was most convenient. They built this one in the 4th century BC, digging into the hillside to excavate the *cavea*, or seating area, but the Romans almost entirely rebuilt it in the 1st–3rd centuries, adding the *scena* (the columns and niches of the stage area) and digging a trench in the orchestra to hold the animals and fighters used for their gladiatorial displays. You can walk freely around, puzzling out how the audience entered through the three arched gates, once faced in marble, tracing the *proscenium* (stage) and the *parascenia* (wings), before scrambling up the *cavea* and testing its famous acoustical properties – or alternatively, catch a summer performance here during the arts festival (➤ 22), and you'll see what the fuss is about. Come early or late to avoid the huge crowds of day visitors and coach parties.

Walking in the footsteps of ancient audiences

Valle dei Templi, Agrigento

The finest Greek temples in Italy, glowing golden in the sun, are strung along an idyllic olive-planted ridge beside the sea.

Founded in 580 BC, Greek Agrigento was a rich colony, the profits of its wars and trade funding the building of fabulous temples. These lie in two zones in the so-called Valle dei Templi, below the 'modern' town of Agrigento (▶ 24). The east zone is traversed by the ancient via Sacra, along which lie the 67m (221 feet) long Temple of Herakles (500 BC), the honey-gold Temple of Concord and the stately Temple of Hera (450 BC), a half-ruined structure whose walls still show the red marks of the fire that destroyed much of the city in 406 BC. The stunningly serene and balanced Temple of Concord, once faced with brilliantly painted marble and still one of the best preserved Greek temples in the world, owes its superb condition to its conversion in the 6th century into a Christian church. It was built about 430 BC and has 34 Doric columns, surmounted at each end by a perfectly preserved entablature.

The west zone contains the ruins of the Temple of Olympian Zeus, the largest Greek temple in the world, which once covered an area larger than a football field. The vast toppled figure (telamon) that lies on the ground (▶ 36) is one of a series which supported the architrave of the temple; its dimensions give an idea of the size of the building. Beyond this are more excavations, including the four columns of the so-called Temple of Castor and Pollux, a 19th-century reconstruction.

INFORMATION

 B3
Valle dei Templi
✉ Valle dei Templi
☎ 0922 621 611;
www.parcovalledeitempli.it
🕐 Apr–Sep daily 9–6;
Oct–Mar daily 9–4
🍴 At entrance and kiosk on site €
♿ Poor
💶 €€€
↔ Agrigento (▶ 24); Museo Nazionale Archeológico, Agrigento (▶ 36)
❓ All the temples are floodlit every evening

Columns of the Temple of Herakles

Villa Romana del Casale, Piazza Armerina

INFORMATION

+ C3
- Villa Romana del Casale, Piazza Armerina
- 0935 686 667; info 333 190 7185
www.villaromana delcasale.it (Italian only)
- May–Sep 8–6, ticket office closes at 5; Oct–Apr daily 8–4:30 ticket office closes at 3:30
- Restaurant (€€)and bar (€) just outside main entrance
- Linea; from Piazza Armerina May–Sep 9, 10, 11, 1, 4 & 5; return service on half hour from 9:30
- €€€
- Poor
- Enna

Detail of the incredible mosaic floor

The enormous ruins of this magnificent Roman villa boast the finest Roman mosaics in situ anywhere in the Roman world.

The Villa Romana was probably built towards the end of the 3rd century AD, the main house of a huge estate whose owner was likely to have been a member of the imperial family. Every floor surface in this vast and luxurious property, excavated in the 1920s, is magnificently decorated – with hunting scenes, stories from classical myths and references to everyday life.

Walkways run round the interior, from which you can examine all 40 mosaics from a raised vantage point. The route first takes you past the baths, then in through the vestibule to the peristyle, the open courtyard garden that was the centre of all Roman villas. From here you'll reach a series of bedchambers before viewing the Hall of the Small Hunt, a jolly scene of the villa owner enjoying the chase and the picnic after it. Next, steps ascend to the 60m (200 foot) long Hall of the Great Hunt, the focal point of the villa, whose extraordinary mosaics illustrate a wonderful series of hunting scenes, complete with African species, and galleys travelling across an ocean packed with fish. From here you'll come to what is, perhaps, Casale's most famous mosaic, the Bikini Girls, ten scantily dressed maidens engaged in gymnastics. Near here is the triclinium, the banqueting hall, whose pavements show scenes from the Labours of Hercules. Don't miss the so-called Erotic Chamber – pretty mild – and the children's rooms.

SICILY's
best

Sicily's Best

Towns and Villages

In the Top 25

1 **AGRIGENTO** (➤ 24)
2 5 **PALERMO** (➤ 25, 28)
6 **CEFALÙ** (➤ 30)
7 **MONREALE** (➤ 30)
8 **ENNA** (➤ 32)
9 **ERICE** (➤ 33)
10 **MARSALA** (➤ 34)
11 **MAZARA DEL VALLO** (➤ 35)
15 **NOTO** (➤ 38)
16 17 **SIRACUSA** (➤ 39, 40)
18 **RAGUSA** (➤ 41)
20 **CALTAGIRONE** (➤ 43)
22 **TAORMINA** (➤ 45)

SICILY'S ISLANDS

North, west and south of Sicily lie its islands: the Aeolian, the Egadi, Ustica, Pantelleria and the Pelagie, tiny archipelagos that pull in the summer crowds seeking sun, sea, natural beauty and laid-back pleasures. Tourism is important, but so too is fishing, for the waters round these islands are among the cleanest and most abundant in the Mediterranean. Throw in some impressive natural phenomena in the shape of a couple of active volcanoes, some rich history and archaeological treasure, and the islands become a whole destination in themselves

Fishing boats at Castellamare del Golfo

CASTELLAMMARE DEL GOLFO

Castellammare del Golfo, the ancient harbour for the classical city of Segesta (➤ 44), crouches beneath the hills on the Golfo del Castellammare. This busy fishing port, with wide quays below the remains of an Aragonese castle, reputedly inspired Mario Puzo's novel, *The Godfather*.

+ A2 **|1|** Bars and restaurants in town **|R|** Castellammare del Golfo **|↔|** Segesta (➤ 44) **|i|** via A de Gasperi 6 **|☎|** 0924 592 111; www.castellammaredelgolfo.com **|◷|** Mon, Wed Fri 9–2, Tue & Thu 9–2, 4–6

CATANIA

Unashamedly commercial, Catania is Sicily's second city, an ancient settlement that thrived under the Romans. It's a dour, forbidding place, overshadowed by Etna. Ravaged by eruption and earthquake, the city has been rebuilt over the centuries, most notably after the 1693 'quake when Vaccarini's architecture transformed it into a showcase baroque city.

+ D3 **|1|** Bars and restaurants in town **|R|** Catania **|↔|** Mount Etna (➤ 35) **|?|** Driving into Catania is not advised **|i|** via D Cimarosa 10 **|☎|** 0957 306 211; www.apt.catania.it; www.comune.catania.it **|◷|** Mon–Fri 9–8; Sat–Sun 9–2

COMISO

For some low-key baroque pleasures head for Comiso, rebuilt after the 1693 earthquake, though still retaining the medieval castle built by its overlords, the powerful Naselli family. Pick of its churches is the Santissima Annunziata (1772–93), crowned with a beautiful blue dome, from where you can walk downhill to the other main church, Santa Maria delle Stelle. Nearby, the waters that feed the fountain in the Piazza Fonte Diana were used by the Romans in their bathhouse.

+ C4 **|1|** Bars and restaurants in town **|R|** Cómiso **|↔|** Ragusa; www.ragusa-sicilia.it/english

MESSINA

Ancient Messina, inhabited for nearly 3,000 years, overlooks the straits that divide Sicily from mainland

Italy. Repeatedly damaged by earthquakes, Sicily's third largest city spreads around a sickle-shaped harbour, a stone's throw from the Duomo (Cathedral), whose campanile houses one of world's largest astronomical clocks.

🚩 D1 🍴 Bars and restaurants in town 🚇 Messina 🏢 Piazza della Repubblica, ☎ 0906 72944; www.comune.messina.it
🕐 Mon–Thu 8:30–1, 3–5, Fri 8:30–1

MODICA

Built after the 1693 earthquake, Modica is a lovely town, its houses scrambling up the steep slopes and its main thoroughfares wide and elegant. These, Corso Umberto and via Giarratana, cover two torrential rivers and were laid out after the 1902 floods. Most of the monuments are ranged along the Corso, while a flight of steps leads up to San Pietro (1698), and higher still, reached by some 250 steps, the church of San Giorgio.

🚩 D4 🍴 Bars and restaurants in town 🚇 Modica 🔁 Ragusa (➤ 41); Noto (➤ 38) 🏢 Piazza Monumento, Corso Umberto 1 ☎ 0932 753 324 🕐 Apr–Sep daily 9–1, 4–8; Oct–Mar daily 9–1, 3:30–7:30

SCIACCA

Spa town and vibrant fishing port, lovely Sciacca has plenty of low-key Mediterranean charm. Head through the Porta San Salvatore in the upper town's encircling walls to walk down the Corso Vittorio Emanuele to Piazza Scandaliato, the place for the *passeggiata*. If you're heading for the beach, the best bets are San Marco and the Contrada Sobareto; in spring, Sciacca has one of the best carnivals in Sicily.

🚩 B3 🍴 Bars and restaurants in town 🚇 Sciacca 🔁 Agrigento (➤ 24) 🎭 Carnevale for the week before Ash Wednesday
🏢 Corso Vittorio Emanuele 84 ☎ 0925 227 44;
www.aziendaturismosciacca.it 🕐 Mon–Sat 8–2, 4–6

TRAPANI

Old Trapani (Greek drepanon means sickle) occupies a curving, narrow spit of land, with miles of saltpans stretching to the south. It has traditionally made its money from tuna – canned tuna was invented here – salt and carved coral but today only the salt industry remains, though its ferry port is still busy. This is one of western Sicily's most handsome towns, with a wide waterfront and a general air of discreet prosperity. The town's highlights include the splendid baroque churches and palazzi along the Corso Vittorio Emanuele, the main drag, and the Santuario dell'Annunziata (Sanctuary of the Annunciation).

🚩 A2 🍴 Bars and restaurants in town 🚇 Trápani 🚢 Ferries to Isole Egadi 🔁 Marsala (➤ 33); Museo Whitaker, Mòzia (➤ 37) www.apt.trapani.it 🎭 Carnevale for the week before Ash Wednesday
🏢 Piazza Garibaldi ☎ 0923 29000 🕐 Sep–Jun Mon–Sat 8:30–1:30, 2:30–7:30, Sun 9–12; Jul & Aug Mon–Sat 8–2, 2:30 8, Sun 9–1

BAROQUE ARCHITECTURE

There's ebullient and ornate baroque architecture all over Europe, but nowhere is it better seen than in Sicily, where entire town centres are a glorious parade of design, gaiety and ostentation. Born in Rome in the late 16th century, full-blown baroque style reached Sicily some 50 years later, where it was transformed into something unique, a fusion of planning, architecture and ornamentation. It's seen at its best in the towns of southeast Sicily, though you'll find baroque churches and palazzi in almost every town.

The Dome of Santa Maria delle Stelle, Comiso

Best Museums & Archaeological Sites

ENJOY YOUR VISIT

If you're visiting archaeological sites in summer, bear in mind that many are very exposed to the sun; visit early or late in the afternoon, wear a hat and take water as you explore. Many sites were entire cities and are very large, so comfortable shoes make sense too.

MUSEO DELLE MARIONETTE, PALERMO

Puppet theatre is a traditional Sicilian entertainment, and this fascinating museum, founded in 1975, preserves over 3,500 puppets and stages shows. The puppets, 80cm (31 inches) tall and fully articulated and dressed in rich costumes, are used to enact tales of chivalry and exploits of saints and bandits.

➕ B1 ✉ Piazzetta Niscemi 5 (via Butera) ☎ 091 328 060; www.museomarionettepalermo.it 🕐 Daily 9–1, Mon–Fri 3:30–6:30 🍴 Cafés in Piazza Marina 🎫 €€ ♿ Fair 🔄 Cappella Palatina (➤ 25); Cattedrale (➤ 28), San Cataldo (➤ 54); La Martorana (➤ 54); San Francesco d'Assisi (➤ 54), all in Palermo 🚌 Tourist bus Linea A + 103, 105, 139, 824

GALLERIA REGIONALE SICILIANA, PALERMO

Palazzo Abatellis (1488) houses Sicily's finest art collection, with two floors crammed with the cream of the island's medieval sculpture and painting. The ground floor is almost exclusively devoted to sculpture, but one of the first rooms contains the remarkable 15th-century Triumph of Death, probably by a Flemish painter, and Francesco Laurana's serene portrait Bust of Eleonora d'Aragona. Upstairs, there's a representative collection of early Sicilian art.

➕ B1 ✉ via Alloro 4 ☎ 091 623 0011 🕐 Mon, Fri, Sat & Sun 9–1, Tue–Thu 9–1, 2:30–7 🍴 Trattoria Stella, via Alloro 104 🚌 Tourist bus Line A + 103, 105, 139 ♿ Fair 🎫 €€€ 🔄 Cappella Palatina (➤ 25); Cattedrale (➤ 28); Catacombe dei Cappuccini (➤ 26)

Greek artefacts in the Museo Archeológico, Palermo

MUSEO ARCHEOLÓGICO, PALERMO

An ex-convent houses one of Italy's best archaeological museums, with superb Greek pieces, including a massive Gorgon's head from Selinunte (➤ 53) and 19 snarling lion's-head waterspouts from Himera. Beyond these are a magnificent collection of metopes (Doric Greek stone temple reliefs) from Selinunte and a fine Etruscan collection. Upstairs, there are some exceptional Hellenistic pieces, including a bronze ram from Siracusa (➤ 40).

➕ B1 ✉ piazza Olivella 24 ☎ 091 611 6805;

www.regione.sicilia.it/beniculturali/dirbenicult/salinas
🕐 Mon 8:30–1:45, Tue–Sat 8:30–6:45 🍴 Bars on Piazza Verdi
♿ Fair 💶 €€ 🔁 Cappella Palatina (➤ 25); Cattedrale (➤ 28)
🚌 Tourist bus Linea A + 101, 102, 103, 104

TINDARI

Founded in 396 BC, the Greek settlement of Tindari continued to thrive under Roman rule, and much of the excavations date from Roman times. Star turns include the partially restored 4th-century basilica, the vibrant mosaics in the bath complex, and two luxurious houses. Don't miss the late 4th century BC theatre, adapted for Roman gladiatorial displays.
🔲 D1 ✉ Tindari ☎ 3389 928 453 🕐 Jan–Feb, Nov–Dec 9–4; Mar & Oct 9–5; Apr–Aug 9–7; Sep 9–6 ♿ Poor 💶 €

ERACLEA MINOA

Eraclea Minoa stands on a ridge above the sea with an arc of sand backed by pines on one side and the mouth of the River Platani on the other. The remnants of this 6th-century BC settlement are still largely unexcavated, but the massive city walls still stand, as does the theatre, first built in the 4th century BC and restored by the Romans 700 years later.
🔲 B3 ✉ Eraclea Minoa 🕐 9–1 hour before dusk ♿ Fair 💶 €
🔁 Agrigento (➤ 24)

SELINUNTE

Mighty Selinus was founded around 650 BC by Greek settlers and virtually destroyed in 409 BC. One area of the vast site contains the eastern temples, known only as E, F and G. The most complete is Doric Temple E, reconstructed in 1958; it was probably dedicated to Aphrodite. Temple F, behind it, is the oldest, dating from around 550 BC, while G, save for one solitary column a vast heap of jumbled stones, was Zeus' shrine. To the west, the acropolis has been excavated and contains city streets, sections of walls and five other temples.
🔲 C5 ✉ Selinunte ☎ 0924 46277; www.selinunte.net
🕐 Apr–Sep daily 9–6; Sep–Mar daily 9–4 🍴 Bar at site entrance
♿ Visitor centre good, site poor 💶 €€€ 🔁 Mazara del Vallo (➤ 34)

MUSEO ARCHEOLÓGICO PAOLO ORSI, SIRACUSA

The Museo Archeológico Paolo Orsi is a scholarly museum, tracing the history of both the pre-Greek and Greek civilisations on Sicily, with copious exhibits, plans, photographs and models. Amongst the sculpture, the exquisite Landolina Venus, a Roman copy of a Hellenistic piece found in the grounds of the museum, stands out.
🔲 D3 ✉ viale Teocrito 66 ☎ 0931464 022 🕐 Tue–Sat 9–7, Sun 9–1 ♿ Good 💶 €€€ 🔁 Parco Archeológico della Neapolis (➤ 40); Catacombs (➤ 27); Ortygia (➤ 39), Duomo (➤ 54), all in Siracusa

IN RESTAURO

In restauro – in restoration; these words are essential vocabulary for museum visitors in Italy, where museums, archaeological sites and churches often mysteriously close for no apparent reason, sometimes for days, sometimes for years on end. Even if a museum is open, you may find some sections closed, or visitors hustled out before official closing times. Don't be surprised, and if you are making a special trip to see something specific, phone ahead before you set off. Bear in mind too, that tourist websites are often out of date as far as opening hours are concerned.

Remains of Temple E at Selinunte, dedicated to Aphrodite

53

Churches

THE ART OF MOSAIC

Mosaics are designed to cover large surfaces like a skin, and are composed of thousands of tiny pieces of coloured glass, fitted together to form a picture. They are created by first plastering an area, then tracing the design in fine detail. Each day, a layer of cement is applied and the *tesserae*, glass pieces, are embedded in it. Glass of all colours is used, including gold and silver, made by applying the metals in leaf form to transparent glass, then fusing them with an over-layer. The glass shards are deliberately set at different angles so the light will be refracted in varying ways.

Intricately carved façade of the Duomo, Siracusa

> **In the Top 25**
>
> **5** CATTEDRALE, PALERMO (➤ 28)
> **6** DUOMO, CEFALÙ (➤ 29)
> **7** DUOMO, MONREALE (➤ 30)

DUOMO, SIRACUSA

No other building in Sicily illustrates the island's layers of civilisation better than Siracusa's Duomo, built where the goddess Athena's shrine once stood and incorporating the Doric columns of the pagan temple. The temple was converted into a Christian church and became the cathedral in 640. Its ebullient façade was added after the 1693 earthquake, and contrasts with the austere interior.

🕂 D3 ⊠ Piazza del Duomo ☎ 0931 65328 🕐 Daily 7:30–6 except during services 👢 Free ⟷ Parco Archeológico della Neapolis (➤ 40); Catacombs (➤ 27); Ortygia (➤ 39); Duomo (➤ 53); Museo Archeológico Paolo Orsi (➤ 53), all in Siracusa

SAN CATALDO, PALERMO

San Cataldo, topped by three squat little red domes, was founded in 1154 by Maio of Bari, chancellor to William I. Maio died in 1160, leaving the interior undecorated. The plain altar is original, as is the beautiful Arabic mosaic pavement.

🕂 B1 ⊠ Piazza Bellini 3 ☎ 338 722 8775 🕐 Mon–Fri 9:30–1, 3:30–6; Sat & Sun 9:30–1 🚌 Tourist bus Linea A + 101, 102, 103, 104 👢 Poor 👢 € ⟷ Cappella Palatina (➤ 25); Cattedrale (➤ 28)

LA MARTORANA, PALERMO

The Martorana was founded around 1146 and given in 1233 to the nuns of the Marturanu convent. The interior of the church was decorated with dazzling mosaics; those of the dome, the apse, the side vaults and two panels at the back remain.

🕂 B1 ⊠ Piazza Bellini 3 ☎ 091 616 1692 🕐 Mon–Sat 8–1, 3:30–7 🚌 Tourist bus Linea A + 101, 102, 103, 104 👢 Poor 👢 Free ⟷ Cappella Palatina (➤ 25); Cattedrale (➤ 28)

SAN FRANCESCO D'ASSISI, PALERMO

The 13th-century church is one of the few in Palermo whose interior has been returned to its original appearance. Step through its zig-zag portal, topped by a magnificent rose window, and you'll find yourself in a simple interior. The chapels on the left are *quattrocento*; the fourth is the island's first example of Renaissance art.

🕂 B1 ⊠ Piazza San Francesco 🕐 Daily 9–12, 4–6:30 👢 Free 🚌 Tourist bus Linea A + 101,102 ⟷ Cappella Palatina (➤ 25); Cattedrale (➤ 28); Galleria Regionale Siciliane (➤ 52); Museo Archeológico (➤ 52); Museo delle Marionette (➤ 52); San Cataldo (➤ 54); La Martorana (➤ 54), all in Palermo

Seaside Towns and Beaches

GIARDINI-NAXOS
The beautiful sands and clear waters of Giardini-Naxos, Sicily's fastest-growing resort, draw thousands of summer visitors, who flock here for its modern hotels, true Sicilian atmosphere and beach-life. Accommodation and restaurants are good, and there are convenient transport links to Taormina (➤ 45).
🚕 D2 ✉ Giardini-Naxos 🍴 Numerous bars and restaurants in town; beach cafés and bars 🚉 Taormina/Giardini-Naxos 🚌 Taormina (➤ 45); Mazzarò (➤ 55); Mount Etna (➤ 35) 🛈 via Tysandros 54 ☎ 0942 51010; www.aastgiardininaxos.it 🕐 Mon–Fri 8:30–2, 4–7, Sat 8:30–2

MAZZARÒ, TAORMINA
Tight against the hillside that slopes precipitously down from Taormina lie the twin *lidi* (resorts) of Mazzarò and Spisone, the nearest beaches to the town. Mazzarò has twin beaches on curving bays overlooking the islet of Isola Bella, connected to the shore by a strand of shingle, while north lies Spisone. The coast is a marine-life sanctuary and the snorkelling excellent.
🚕 D2 ✉ Mazzarò 🍴 Beach bars and restaurants 🚉 Taormina
❓ A *funivia* (cable-car) connects Mazzarò with Taormina

MONDELLO
Escape the heat and noise of Palermo by heading the 11km (7 miles) round the looming bulk of Monte Pellegrino to the long, curving sandy beach of Mondello, Palermo's playground par excellence. Packed every weekend, Mondello has all the necessities for a lazy beach day – clean sand, clear sea and beachside restaurants serving the freshest of fish, while after dark it's renowned for its open-air discos.
🚕 B1 ✉ Mondello 🍴 Beach bars and restaurants; restaurants in town 🚌 806, 833 (833 is summer only)

SAN VITO LO CAPO
For centuries, coral and tuna fishing brought in the money to the remote village of San Vito, but the 20th century saw the start of the tourist boom, as Italians discovered its stunning beaches. In high summer, they come in droves to stroll the neat 18th-century streets and lie on the beach, but outside high season, you'll have the town virtually to yourself.
🚕 A1 ✉ San Vito lo Capo 🛈 Museo del Mare, via Savoia 57/via Venza 12 ☎ 0923 972464; www.sanvitoweb.com 🕐 May–Sep daily approx 9–1, 8–12

BEACH ACCESS

By law, a section of all Italian beaches has to be open to the public, but most holidaymakers prefer to patronise one of the privately run *stabilimenti*, stretches of enclosed beach with sun beds, umbrellas, showers, changing rooms and a bar or restaurant. Most have their own lifeguards. Prices vary depending on the facilities but you should reckon on around €10–15 per day, with reduced rates for three days or longer.

Beach life is good at Giardini-Naxos

Wild Places

HIKING

The concept of hiking is relatively new in Sicily and the network of paths still fairly rudimentary. You can pick up maps for the Madonie, but don't expect them to be accurate – paths may peter out or even plunge over a precipice. Always be well prepared at altitude, with suitable boots and clothing and take food and plenty of water with you; if the weather looks dubious don't go; mountain rescue services are non-existent.

Gorge and waterfall at Gole dell'Alcántara

In the Top 25

12 MOUNT ETNA (➤ 35)
13 RISERVA NATURALE DELLO ZINGARO (➤ 42)

GOLE DELL'ALCÁNTARA

The lovely Alcántara gorge, with its clear water and extraordinary stone formations, runs inland just south of Taormina, a 19m (64 foot) deep cleft carved by the river Alcántara through the hardened basalt of one of Etna's ancient eruptions. Explore it by taking a lift down to the narrowest point, the *Gole* (throat), donning protective clothing – the water's freezing – and scrambling along the river bed to the waterfall.

🔢 D2 🕐 Lift May–Sep 7:30–8; Oct–Apr 7:30–7 🍴 Bar and restaurant on upper level 🚹 Poor 🎫 Lift to bottom of gorge €2.50 rubber boot and salopette hire €15 🔄 Taormina (➤ 45); Mount Etna (➤ 35); Giardini-Naxos (➤ 55)

MONTI MADONÍE

The high mountains to the south of Cefalù form the Madonie range, since 1989 the Parco Naturale delle Madonie. Rising to over 1,900m (5,700 feet), this is a marvellous swathe of upland country, dotted with beguiling villages and criss-crossed with hiking trails, riding and mountain-bike routes; details are available at the park office.

🔢 C2 ✉ Ente Parco delle Madonie, Corso Paolo Agliata 16, Petralia Sottana ☎ 0921 684 011; www.parcodellemadonie.it 🔄 Cefalù (➤ 29); Petralia Soprana (➤ 15)

PARCO NATURALE DI VENDICARI

The Riserva di Vendicari, in southeast Sicily, is a flat, coastal nature reserve centred around a chain of three lagoons. These are one of Sicily's most important feeding grounds during the spring migration, attracting many rare species, including resident flamingos.

🔢 D4 ✉ Ufficio Provinciale dell'Azienda FF.DD, via San Giovanni all Catacombe, Siracusa ☎ 0931 67450; www.parks.it/riserva.oasi.vendicari 🔄 Noto (➤ 38)

MONTI NEBRODI

The Parco dei Nebrodi is a high upland area (1,200–1,500m/3,900–4,900 feet) with Sicily's richest forest and woodland. The landscape is more varied than the Madonie, with thick forests, upland pastureland, woods high peaks, all good places for spotting wildlife. The Nebrodi are well-watered with streams and lakes – head for the beautiful Biviere di Cesarò for great birdlife and fabulous views to Etna.

🔢 C2 ✉ Ente Parco delle Nebrodi, via Bellini 79, Cesarò; via Latteri, San Fratello ☎ Cesarò 095 773 2061; San Fratello 0941 799 651; www.parcodeinebrodi.it

Free Attractions

Ceramic artefact, Cefalù

BEACHES

Every resort has one stretch of beach with free access, while remote beaches, in the coastal nature reserves in particular, are wonderfully deserted and free. You'll need to take your own beach stuff.

FESTIVALS

Every Sicilian town and village celebrates its patron saint's feast day with a *festa*, involving parades, music, eating, drinking and entertainment – local tourist offices will have details.

FOOD FESTIVALS

Check out local tourist offices, posters and flyers for details of local *sagre*, food festivals devoted to the speciality of a particular area. These can range from wine, olive oil and cheese to fish, sausages, pistachio nuts and even capers. *Sagre* usually involve communal tables, bands, parades, and fireworks.

MARKETS

You don't have to buy to enjoy Sicily's colourful markets – check out the big daily ones in Palermo (► 25) and other major towns, and look out for the weekly markets held everywhere.

PARKS

Access to Sicily's beautiful natural parks (► 20) is free; check out Italy's park portal, www.parks.it, to get the lowdown.

THE *PASSEGGIATA*

Join the evening *passeggiata*, a quintessential Sicilian experience. Between 6 and 9 or so the main streets and piazza are full of locals strolling and meeting friends, with everyone spruced up for the occasion.

BUDGET ACCOMMODATION

If you're travelling on a budget, self-catering is often a good option. Outside July and August there's normally little need to book ahead; tourist offices will have lists of what's available. Other possibilities include private rooms (*affita camara*) and camping.

EATING AND DRINKING CHEAPLY

If the weather's fine you can put together a delicious picnic of local produce, fruit and salads – the best places for budget shopping are the daily or weekly markets and supermarkets. For restaurant eating, head for a pizzeria, where you'll rarely have to pay over €10 for a superb pizza and something to drink. If you're drinking in a bar, remember that it's far cheaper to stand at the bar – a seat at a table automatically hoiks up the price, particularly in popular tourist towns and resorts.

For Children

ACQUAPARK PARADISE CITY

This big water park near Siracusa has got the lot – wave machines, slides, flumes, toddlers' pool, and waterfalls. It can get very crowded in July and August, particularly at weekends.

🞧 D3 ⊠ Località Spalla 1 ☎ 0931 761 474 ⏱ Daily mid-Jun to mid-Sep 💶 €€€

ACQUARIO, SIRACUSA

There are three rooms in this attraction, where kids can gaze at both Mediterranean and tropical fish. There's a good selection of shells on display and older children will enjoy the papyrus that grows in the Fonte Aretusa outside – local artisans still use it for paper-making and basket work.

🞧 D3 ⊠ Villetta Aretusa al Foro Vittorio Emanuele II, Siracusa ☎ 0931 167 4461 ⏱ Daily 10–7 💶 €€

BEACHES AND SWIMMING

There are beaches all around the coast of Sicily, ranging from gently sloping sand to rocky coves and inlets. Some are remote and entail a walk to get there, others fully developed with every amenity. If you have small children it makes sense to book into a *stabilimento* (➤ 55) for the day, where you'll have access to shade, showers and a life guard will be on duty. Many holiday complexes offer water sports for older children, including sailing tuition, scuba courses and jet skis, and many are open to non-residents – tourist offices will advise. Many hotels have their own pools.

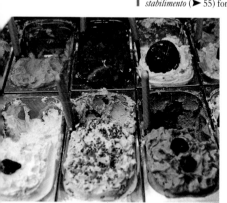

CATACOMBS AND MUMMIES

Older children will be enthralled by the catacombs at Siracusa (➤ 27) and the mummified corpses in the Catacombe dei Cappuccini in Palermo (➤ 26).

Ice cream in flavours to tempt every palate

CITTÀ DEL MARE

This holiday complex has an excellent water park, with slides descending from the pools down the cliffs into the sea. They have a full programme of water-based sports, plus sailing tuition and scuba courses.

🞧 D2 ⊠ SS 113, Terrasini www.cittadelmare.it ⏱ Daily Jun–Sep

ETNALAND

Sicily's top kids' park has plenty of dinosaurs, zoo animals and other attractions including its main draw, the water park, complete with slides, wave machines, helter-skelters, waterfalls and flumes.

➕ D2/D3 ✉ SS 121 (take exit Misterbianco off A 19 near Catania)
☎ 095 989 7101/102; www.parcozoo.it 🕐 Daily Mar–Sep 9–4
(times may alter, see website) 💷 €€€

EXPLORING CASTLES
If you're sightseeing, take in a castle where the kids can exercise both bodies and imaginations – top draws include the Castello di Lombardia at Enna (➤ 31), the Castello di Venere at Erice (➤ 32), Castello Ventimiglia surrounded by mountains at Castelbuono (➤ 15) and Aci Castello, built jutting out above the sea between Catania and Taormina. Other children will enjoy archeological sites, which all have plenty of space to run around. Top of the list are Mòzia (➤ 37), reached by ferry across a lagoon, Agrigento (➤ 24), for sheer scale, and Siracusa (➤ 27), for the theatre and quarries.

ICE CREAM
If things look bad, a Sicilian ice cream will soon stop the tears and soothe the temper. Take your children to a gelateria serving home-made ice cream (*artigianato* or *produzione propria*) and let them load up a cone, and you can rest assured that they're eating a pure product made with natural ingredients and no additives.

MOUNT ETNA
Europe's most active volcano (➤ 35) is a must for children and it's worth splashing out on the trip up the mountain from Rifugio Sapienza (➤ 19) – lava, sulphurous smells and underground rumblings will enthral your kids.

PUPPET THEATRES
It may be in Italian, but children normally enjoy a puppet performance – the best place to catch one is at Palermo's Museo delle Marionette. Even if there's no performance, there are over 3,500 puppets on display and other exhibits as well.

➕ B1 ✉ Piazzetta Niscemi 5 (via Butera), Palermo ☎ 091 328
060; www.museomarionettepalermo.it 🕐 Daily 9–1, Mon–Fri
3:30–6:30 🚌 Tourist bus Linea A + 103, 105, 139, 824 💷 €€

RIDING
You can go riding and trekking in the wonderful scenery of the Madonie mountains, ask at tourist offices or visit the park's information office for further details.

➕ C2 ✉ Ente Parco delle Madonie, Corso Paolo Agliata 16, Petralia
Sottana ☎ 0921 684 011; www.parcodellemadonie.it

Pinocchio marionettes

59

Places to Have Lunch

Seafood salad makes a delicious light lunch

AL COVO DEI BEATI PAOLI (€€)

Sit in or out on one of Palermo's nicest *piazze* and enjoy choosing from the wide menu – excellent seafood and fish, and a great atmosphere.

✚ B1 ✉ Piazza Marina 50, Palermo ☎ 091 616 6634; www.alcovodeibeatipaoli.com

ANTICA FOCCACERIA SAN FRANCESCO (€)

For a real taste of Palermo, come to this traditional eating place, established in 1834, to eat superb *pizze* or some of the great range of traditional Palermitanan fast food at the marble-topped tables.

✚ B1 ✉ via Alessandro Paternostro 58, Palermo ☎ 091 320 264

CANTINACCIA (€€)

This well-priced, down-to-earth restaurant has a summer veranda overlooking the sea – help yourself from the antipasto buffet before moving on to fresh fish and real Sicilian desserts.

✚ D3 ✉ via XX Settembre 13, Siracusa ☎ 0931 165 945

LA BOTTE (€–€€)

Sit with the crowds of locals on Taormina's liveliest square to enjoy *cucina tipica siciliana* and *pizze*.

✚ D2 ✉ Piazza San Domenico 4, Taormina ☎ 0942 24198

MONTE SAN GIULIANO (€€€)

You can eat in or outside in the courtyard at this fine restaurant in the heart of beautiful Erice, where local produce is lovingly cooked with a modern twist.

✚ A2 ✉ Vicolo San Rocco 7, Erice ☎ 0923 869 595; www.montesangiuliano.it

OSTARIA DEL DUOMO (€€)

Sit on one of Sicily's loveliest piazzas and gaze at the Duomo while you enjoy good local cooking with the accent on fish.

✚ C2 ✉ via Seminario 5, Cefalù ☎ 0921 421 838

PIERROT (€€)

Grab a table overlooking the beach in this light and airy restaurant and enjoy super-fresh seafood and fish; the lunchtime set menu represents excellent value.

✚ A3 ✉ via Marco Polo 108, Marinella di Selinunte ☎ 0924 46205

TRATTORIA LA RUOTA (€€)

Near the Villa Romana, this nice restaurant serves good inland cooking, featuring home-made pasta with meat sauces, local rabbit and veal.

✚ C3 ✉ Contrada Paratore Casale, Piazza Armerina ☎ 0935 680 542; www.trattorialaruota.it

Grilled breaded cuttlefish is especially tasty eaten overlooking the sea

SICILY
where to...

Palermo and the North Coast

PRICES

Approximate prices for a three-course meal for one, excluding drinks and service:

€ = under €20
€€ = €20–€35
€€€ = over €35

SICILIAN FOOD

Sicilian cooking reflects the island's history, with culinary influences from its waves of Greek, Arab, and Norman invaders. As throughout all Italy, it's an intensely regional cuisine, with the emphasis on seasonal, fresh produce of the highest quality. Flavours are intense, the long-lasting Arabic legacy seen in every type of dish, making Sicilian food spicier, hotter and sweeter than anywhere else in Italy. The staples are bread, pasta, fish and vegetables, the embellishments an astounding array of sweets and *pasticceria*.

CEFALÙ

GABBIANO (€€)
A pretty seafront restaurant cooking classic Sicilian dishes with the accent on fish; family-run and friendly. Pizza oven operates in the evening.
✉ Lungomare Giardina 17
☎ 0921 421 495

L'ANTICA CORTE (€€)
This elegant little courtyard restaurant opposite the Duomo offers home-made dishes using fresh, local ingredients and plenty of vegetables; they have good pizzas if you're watching the budget.
✉ Corso Ruggero 193
☎ 0921 423 228

LA BRACE (€€)
Cosy restaurant in the old town with a long, mixed menu featuring fish and traditional Sicilian dishes alongside rabbit, spicy chicken and delicious desserts.
✉ via XXV Novembre 10
☎ 0921 423 570

LO SCOGLIO UBRIACO (€€€)
The 'Drunken Rock' is a big, bustling fish and seafood restaurant, where everything's cooked to order. Patronised by Italian celebrities who enjoy the terrace above the sea.
✉ via Corso Bordanaro 2–4
☎ 0921 423 370

MOVÈ (€€)
Tiny and unpretentious restaurant on the lungomare, serving excellent antipasti, fresh fish and mouthwatering puddings. Excellent value tourist menu.
✉ via Lungomare Giardina 10–11 ☎ 0921 421 901

OSTARIA DEL DUOMO (€€)
Lovely restaurant with terrace overlooking the Duomo, which offers Sicilian cooking with the accent on seafood – superb prawns and seafood pasta.
✉ via Seminario 5
☎ 0921 421 838

MONDELLO

CHARLESTON (€€€)
Famous and upmarket seafront restaurant in an art nouveau building, where the accent's on fish. Sample the house style via the tasting menu; exceptional wine list.
✉ viale Regina Elena
☎ 091 450 171

LA LOCANDA (€)
You may have to queue for a table at this lively pizzeria, which doubles as a bar and pub – locals rate it highly and the atmosphere is great.
✉ via Torre Mondello 26
☎ 091 684 0127

PANAREA (€)
Popular pizzeria, haunt of Palermo's gilded youth, with the best pizzas.
✉ Piazzale Giove1
☎ 091 684 1436

MONREALE

DIETRO L'ANGOLO (€–€€)
Enjoy a pizza or a full meal at this good-value

restaurant with its panoramic summer terrace; they also serve drinks and snacks if you don't want a full meal.

✉ via Chiasso Piave 5
☎ 091 670 4067
◉ Open evenings only

TAVERNA DEL PAVONE (€€)

Family-run establishment with genuine, no frills cooking, excellent service and a warm welcome. Sit in or out and enjoy Sicilian specialities.

✉ Vicolo Pensato 18
☎ 091 640 6209;
www.tavernadelpavone.it

PALERMO

AL COVO DEI BEATI PAOLI (€€)

Sit in or out on one of Palermo's nicest *piazze* and enjoy choosing from the wide menu – seafood and fish, meat and vegetarian dishes.

✉ Piazza Marina 50
☎ 091 616 6634;
www.alcovodeibeatipaoli.com

ANTICA FOCCACERIA SAN FRANCESCO (€)

Established in 1834, this traditional eating place, with marble-topped tables, has superb *pizze* and great traditional fast-food specialities, typical of Palermo.

✉ via Alessandro Paternostro 58
☎ 091 320 264

CAPPELLO (€)

Superb *pasticceria* near the Cathedral with a vast range of pastries and cakes made on the premises using the finest ingredients; particularly

noted for chocolate products.

✉ via Colonna Rotta 68
☎ 091 489 601

ILARDO (€)

Palermo's most famous *gelateria*, founded in the 1880s, with a huge range of flavours of both true ice creams and water ices.

✉ Foro Italico 11–12
☎ 091 616 4413

LE TRE SORELLE (€€)

Founded as a market restaurant in 1888 and still thriving, the 'Three Sisters' serves freshly cooked Sicilian food made with fresh ingredients.

✉ via Volturno 110
☎ 091 585 960

NINO MATRANGA (€)

The eponymous Nino invented a creamy sorbet, called *cremoloso*, which he now produces in 32 flavours.

✉ Piazza Gentili 16
☎ 091 300 292

OSTERIA DEI VESPRI (€€–€€€)

Elegant restaurant serving Sicilian cuisine for the 21st century – traditional ingredients served with a modern twist. Tasting menu and great wine list.

✉ Piazza Croce dei Vespri 6
☎ 091 617 1631;
www.osteriadeivespri.it

STELLA (€€–€€€)

Immensely popular restaurant with courtyard, serving good traditional Sicilian cooking, including meat dishes, and a full range of *pizze*.

✉ via Alloro 104
☎ 091 616 1136

COOLING OFF

Gelaterie serve ice cream, one of Sicily's finest products, thought to have originated as far back as Roman times and certainly enjoyed by the Arabs. Look for one that features *produzione propria* (our own production); such establishments will have a large range of both creamy ices and *granita*, a slushy water ice made with lemon, orange, coffee or seasonal fruit, very refreshing in summer. Don't be surprised to see Sicilians eating a breakfast roll filled with ice cream – why not try it yourself?

FRUTTI DI MARTORANA

Every *pasticceria* worth its salt in the city and province of Palermo displays hand-made *frutti di Martorana*, astonishingly realistic, highly coloured, marzipan fruits. The name comes from the church of the Martorana, whose nuns once raised a little hard cash by the sale of these sweetmeats from the church door. Strawberries, cherries, prickly pears, figs, peaches and apricots are favourites, and you'll often see more exotic creations in the form of prawns, squid and fish, or even tiny cauliflowers and pods of peas. Made with the finest almonds, egg whites and sugar, the *frutti* are cloyingly sweet, a legacy of Sicily's Moorish past.

63

Eastern Sicily

SICILIAN FAST FOOD

Bars and *rosticcerie* are great places for a quick lunch, and you'll find Sicily's answers to the hamburger at all of them. Top of the list are *arancini*, deep-fried, breadcrumb-coated balls of rice with a nugget of meat, cheese or savoury vegetables in the centre – the name means 'oranges' and derives from the shape of these delicious morsels. Other options include *pizzette,* miniature pizza, *foccace,* a type of pizza with savoury toppings, *pannini,* rolls stuffed with salami, prosciutto or cheese, *panelle,* chick-pea fritters, *sfincione,* pizza with onions and anchovies and straightforward *tramezzini* (sandwiches) bursting with prawns, egg or ham.

NOTO

BAR GELATERIA CONSTANZA (€)

Come here for some of the best ice creams in Sicily – classic flavours, fruit ices and sorbets, with specialities such as orange, carob and mulberry scented with jasmine.
✉ via Silvio Spaventa
☎ 0931 538 496

CAFFÈ SICILIA (€)

Famous *pasticceria* producing delicious cakes and pastries made using historic recipes from the Noto area – try a tart with sweet pumpkin filling.
✉ Corso Vittorio Emmanuele 125 ☎ 0931 835 013

IL GIGLIO (€€)

Straighforward *trattoria* in a lovely position near the cathedral. Serves typical Sicilian specialities, including delicious home-made pasta.
✉ Piazza Municipio
☎ 0931 838 640;
www.ristoranteilgiglio.com

NEAS (€–€€)

Eat in under the arches or outside under the stars at this good value, old-fashioned *trattoria*, where the pasta is home-made and the fish is fresh.
✉ via Rocca Pirri 30
☎ 0931 573 538

RAGUSA

DA NINO 'TITOS' (€€)

Choose from the full menu, sample the tasting menu or enjoy a one-plate meal at this excellent family-run restaurant specialising in Ragusan dishes.
✉ via Porta Modica 21–31
☎ 0932 651 449;
www.ristorantetitos.com

DUOMO (€€€)

Ragusa's finest restaurant, where wonderful food is elegantly served and beautifully presented in surroundings to match. Expect Sicilian cuisine with a modern twist and wonderful wines.
✉ via Capitano Bocchieri 31, Ragusa Ibla ☎ 0932 651 265;
www.ristoranteduomo.it

ORFEO (€–€€)

Eat here and enjoy the best of excellent-value Ragusan cooking at knock-down prices, with a good selection of home-made pasta dishes, straightforward grilled meat and some fish.
✉ via Sant'Anna 117, Ragusa Superiore ☎ 0932 621 035

RISTORANTE DON SERAFINO (€€€)

Smart and intimate restaurant, housed in an old stable, offering state-of-the-art, light cooking using old traditions and local ingredients. Long and impressive wine list.
✉ via Orfanotrofio 39, Ragusa Ibla ☎ 0932 248 778;
www.locandadonserafino.it

SIRACUSA

DON CAMILLO (€€€)

The famous and prize-winning chef here specialises in pasta, but all food is taken seriously and his touch with *secondi* is equally deft. The wine list is long and interesting.

✉ via Maestranza 96
☎ 0931 67133; www.
ristorantedoncamillosiracusa.it

IL CENACOLO (€€€)

Touristy but fun restaurant set in green garden on Ortygia with firmly Sicilian cuisine, including fish *cuscus* (couscous) and pizza in the evening. Occasional live entertainment.

✉ via del Consiglio Reginale 10
☎ 0931 65099

IL PORTICCIOLO DA PIERO (€–€€)

Excellent value restaurant near the fish market on Ortygia serving the best and freshest of the day's catch – plain grilled fish and no frills.

✉ via Trento 24
☎ 0931 619 14

LA FOGLIA (€€)

Choice of soups and pasta made using fresh seasonal produce make this a good vegetarian option; good grills as well. Delicious home-made desserts.

✉ via Capodieci 31
☎ 0931 66233; www.lafoglia.it

LA SICILIANA (€)

Good budget choice with excellent pizza from the wood-fired oven – there's a choice of more than 50 toppings. You can sit in or out.

✉ via Savoia 17
☎ 0931 68944

SPIZZICA (€–€€)

Nice eating place in the heart of Ortygia which offers a full menu and pizza at both lunch and

dinner and serves snacks late into the evening.

✉ via Castello Maniace 8
☎ 0931 463 637

TRATTORIA ARCHIMEDE (€€–€€€)

Traditional Siracusan restaurant with a fabulous seafood buffet and huge range of fish *secondi* – a must for fish lovers. The pizzeria across the road is run by same owners.

✉ via Gemmellaro 8
☎ 0931 69701;
www.trattoriaarchimede.it

TAORMINA

LA BOTTE (€–€€)

Restaurant featuring *cucina tipica siciliana* and *pizze*, served at outside tables in summer. Very busy and packed with locals; service can be slow.

✉ Piazza San Domenico 4
☎ 0942 24198

CASA GRUGNO (€€€)

A beautiful 16th-century building is home to up-market restaurant serving local and international cuisine – quality ingredients and light and appetising dishes.

✉ via Santa Maria de Greci
☎ 0942 21208;
www.casagrugno.it

RISTORANTE TAORMINA (€€)

Jolly family-run restaurant with high standards and a good range of dishes from Sicily and other parts of Italy. In summer, the terrace overlooks the sea.

✉ Vico Teofane Cerameo 2 (off Piazza IX Aprile) ☎ 0942 24359

HOW TO EAT

Meals in Sicily follow the classic Italian pattern – an *antipasto* (hors d'oeuvres), a *primo*, the starchy dish that fills you up, usually pasta but, in western Sicily often couscous, and then the *secondo*, the main course. This is normally a fish or meat dish, and is served with a *contorno*, a separately priced side dish of vegetables, potatoes or salad. After this comes *il dolce*, pudding, but you'll find restaurants rarely offer much choice as it's customary to eat either fruit or move on to a *pasticceria* for a cake or pastry or head for a *gelateria* to round off your meal with an ice cream. Never feel pressured into eating every course; it's quite acceptable to skip the *antipasti* or the *primo* and just have a main course, or opt for a *primo* with a salad – the choice is yours.

Inland and the South

SICILIAN WINES

Sicilian wines are on the up and up, with local grape varieties such as Nero d'Avolo, Grecanico and Pignatello being used to create modern wines of great quality. Names to look out for include Corvo, Alcamo, Regaleali, Cervasuolo, Etna and Mamertino, all producing both reds and whites. Marsala is Sicily's own fortified wine, ranging from super sweet to almost dry, and Moscato and Passito from Noto and Syracusa are dessert muscats worth trying, as is Averna, a post-prandial *digestivo* from Caltanissetta.

THIRST QUENCHERS

Sicilians drink a lot of mineral water, either *naturale* (flat) or *gassata* (fizzy), and all the international soft drinks are on offer. The local beer is Messina, and you can also find other Italian and international brands and a wide range of spirits. In summer, look out for *tè freddo* (iced tea), flavoured with mint, lemon or peach, *caffè freddo* (iced coffee) and *latte di mandorla*, a refreshing cold drink made with almond paste dissolved in water. Coffee is superb, but there's little hope of a perfect cup of tea (*tè*), the concept of using boiling water being virtually unknown.

AGRIGENTO

ATENEA (€)
The Atenea is a good tourist bet, serving set menus, which include wine, and à la carte meals. Sit outside in the little piazza and enjoy simple pasta followed by grilled meat or fish.
✉ via Ficani 32
☎ 0922 412 366

KALÒS (€€)
City-centre restaurant with a good reputation serving classic Sicilian food, home-made pasta and daily specials.
✉ Piazzale San Calògero
☎ 0922 263 89

LA POSATA DI FEDERICO II (€€€)
Eat in or outside at this quiet restaurant, which serves local dishes and some from northern Italy; good wine list.
✉ Piazza Cavour 19
☎ None

ROSTICCERIA ANTONELLO PALUMBO (€)
Hot dishes, pannini, roast chicken and superb *arancini* are freshly prepared at this great value *rosticceria* – a good budget choice.
✉ Piazza Sinatra 25
☎ 0922 297 65

RUGA REALI (€€–€€€)
Set in medieval Agrigento town, a rustic eating house, with a good range of both fish and meat dishes. Traditional cooking with home-made pasta and excellent *couscous di pesce*, as well as seafood – prawns, shrimp and squid.
✉ Cortile Scribani 8
☎ 0922 203 70

TRATTORIA DEI TEMPLI (€€)
Terracotta floors, vaulted ceilings and imaginative mainly fish- and seafood-based cooking are found in this pretty restaurant in a lovely setting.
✉ via Panoramica dei Templi 15
☎ 0922 403 110;
www.trattoriadeitempli.it

ENNA

ARISTON (€€)
Traditional restaurant serving up excellent pizzas, local meat and unusually in the interior, fish. The pasta is home-made, the meat grilled over charcoal. Outside tables in summer.
✉ via Roma 353
☎ 0935 260 38

CENTRALE (€€–€€€)
Splendid inland cooking is found in this 100-year old family restaurant, which is famed for its antipasto buffet – start your meal by helping yourself to a range of more than twenty vegetable dishes from the central table, a tasty option for vegetarians.
✉ Piazza VI Dicembre 9
☎ 0935 500 963;
www.ristorantecentrale.net

SAN GENNARO (€)
Outdoor tables with a view, great atmosphere and some of the best *pizze* in town – who could ask for more?
✉ via Belvedere Marconi 6
☎ 0935 240 67

PIAZZA ARMERINA

AL FOGHER (€€€)
This one of Sicily's
most famous restaurants,
where you'll find local
ingredients in exciting
combinations based on
traditional dishes and
served with a modern
twist. Wine list and service
are everything you'd
expect. Booking essential.
✉ Strada Statale 117, Contrada
Bellia, Piazza Armerina
☎ 0935 684 123

AL TEATRO (€)
Sit outside at this good
value pizzeria and enjoy
a fantastically crisp pizza
with a wide selection
of toppings.
✉ via del Teatro 6
☎ 0935 856 62

TRATTORIA LA RUOTA
(€€)
Near the Villa Romana,
this nice restaurant serves
good inland cooking,
featuring home-made
pasta with meat sauces,
local rabbit and veal. Not
open in the evenings.
✉ Contrada Paratore Casale,
Piazza Armerina
☎ 0935 680 542

SCIACCA

AL FARO (€€)
Superbly fresh fish is
served at this friendly
restaurant down by the
fish market.
✉ via Porto 25
☎ 0925 253 49

AMADEUS (€€)
This late-opening
restaurant, housed in a
fine old building, serves a
good range of local

specialities, with the
accent on fish
✉ Corso Vittorio Emanuele 111
☎ 0925 232 03

BAR SCANDAGLIA (€)
Sit in the main piazza and
gaze over the port to sea at
Sciacca's most elegant
café, serving *pasticceria*,
light lunches and fabulous
home-made ice cream.
✉ Piazza Scandaliato 5
☎ 0925 216 65

HOSTARIA DEL VICOLO
(€€–€€€)
Restaurant noted for its
fusion of traditional
Sicilian ingredients and
cooking styles with a 21st-
century attitude to food –
try the tasting menu.
Excellent wine list.
✉ Vicolo Sammaritano 10
☎ 0925 230 71;
www.hostariadelvicolo.com

LA LAMPARA (€€)
Join the locals at this
excellent value, jolly fish
restaurant just across the
road from the docks.
✉ Vicolo Caricatore 33
☎ 0925 850 85

LO STERIPINTO (€)
Excellent pizzeria,
normally packed with
young locals, in the
historic centre.
✉ Corso Vittorio Emanuele 228
☎ 0925 231 77

PORTO SAN PAOLO
(€€€)
The terrace overlooks the
sea at this elegant
restaurant where the
cooking combines the best
of both fish and excellent
grilled meats.
✉ Largo San Paolo 1
☎ 0925 279 82

VEGETARIANS

Sicilians have little concept
of vegetarianism, though,
obviously, if you eat fish
there won't be a problem.
Otherwise, check before
ordering that what appears to
be a straightforward non-meat
dish isn't made with *brodo*
(stock) or spiced up with a few
morsels of ham or meat.

Western Sicily

MARSALA WINE

English sailors had traditionally enjoyed a tipple at sea, and wine had, for many years, been fortified with spirits to preserve it during voyages, port being the staple choice. By the 1770s, the English Mediterranean fleets needed a local supply, and John Woodhouse, an English merchant, added alcohol to Marsala wine and shipped it to Liverpool in 1773. It was an immediate success, endorsed, in 1798, by Admiral Nelson himself, who placed a large order. Today, the wine houses retain their English company names, but are mainly Italian owned, and the *baglios* are still prominent buildings in the town. Marsala is sweet and strong – a great dessert wine or pick-me-up.

ERICE

AIDA (€)

This excellent value, friendly restaurant serves straightforward Sicilian dishes and good *pizze* from the wood-fired oven.
✉ via Cesaro 105
☎ 0923 565 454

MONTE SAN GIULIANO (€€€)

You can eat in or outside in the courtyard at this fine restaurant, which prides itself on its use of local produce and adherence to traditional recipes – with a modern twist. Smoked fish platter, seafood heaped high, pasta with sardines, and couscous are all here, but leave a space for the exquisite *cassata*.
✉ Viccolo San Rocco 7
☎ 0923 869 595

LA VETTA DA MARIO (€–€€)

Rustic décor and cheerful clatter in this good budget choice are the prelude to a range of western Sicilian dishes such as *busiati* (pasta with almonds, capers and tomatoes) and fish *cuscus*. The main draw here, though, is the pizza menu, a great range of paper-thin discs from the wood-fired oven.
✉ via G Fontana 5
☎ 0923 869 404

MARIA GRAMMATICO (€)

Erice is famous for its speciality *pasticcerie*, and this is the best place to sample these – browse at the counter before you choose from the feather-light cakes, the mouth-watering *cannoli* (pastry tubes with ricotta and candied fruit), the *cassata* and the myriad almond sweetmeats.
✉ via Vittorio Emanuele 14
☎ 0923 869 390

MARINELLA DI SELINUNTE

PIERROT (€€)

Grab a table near one of the picture windows overlooking the beach in this light, airy restaurant and enjoy super-fresh seafood and fish. If you've never tried *ricci* (sea urchin) this is the place to come, and the set menu at lunchtime represents excellent value.
✉ via Marco Polo 108
☎ 0924 46205

LIDO AZZURRA BAFFO'S (€€)

The sea-facing terrace here is the main attraction and the food's good too, with the accent, as you would expect, firmly on fish. There's a good pasta with *bottarga*, dried tuna roe – follow it up with the day's catch, freshly grilled.
✉ via Marco Polo 51
☎ 0924 46211

MARSALA

IL GALLO A L'INNAMORATA (€€€)

Book ahead to ensure a table at this little restaurant that's noted for the best cooking in Marsala, with imaginative dishes featuring the best of local fish and meat, with excellent pasta, fresh fish and *porchetta* (whole roasted suckling pig).

Superb wine list and very professional service. Evenings only.

✉ via San Bilardello 18
☎ 32929 918 503

TRATTORIA GARIBALDI (€€)

A long-established restaurant in the heart of town, where the accent's on local produce. Order the antipasti to sample as much as possible of the kitchen's range, and finish with a glass of Marsala.

✉ Piazza dell'Addolorata 35
☎ 0923 953 006

SAN VITO LO CAPO

ALFREDO (€€)

Alfredo's pretty terrace overlooks the sea and it's sea produce you'll eat here, including San Vito's speciality *primo*, *busiati alla sanvitese*, home-made pasta with tuna roe.

✉ Contrada Valanga
☎ 0923 972 366

GNA SARA (€–€€)

This *trattoria* is faithful to local dishes, serving good *cuscus di pesce* and the delicious *busiato al pesto trapanese* – home-made pasta with tomato and caper pesto – follow it up with fresh fish or a pizza.

✉ via Duca dergli Abruzzo 8
☎ 0923 972 100

THÀAM (€€€)

Come here to sample western Sicily's Arab influences – *brik*, *tajine* and couscous are served in Moorish surroundings or outside in summer; good Sicilian staples too.

✉ via Duca degli Abruzzi 34
☎ 0923 972 836

TRAPANI

AI LUMI (€€)

This stylish restaurant, with its elegant traditional furnishings, serves local dishes, wines, oil, cheeses and pasta made on the premises – excellent vegetable dishes.

✉ Corso Vittorio Emanuele 75
☎ 0923 872 418; www.ailumi.it

CALVINO ANTICA PIZZERIA DAL 1946 (€)

Come here for Trapani's own speciality pizza, the '*rianata*', cooked without mozzarella but plenty of oregano. If this doesn't appeal, there's a huge choice of toppings.

✉ via N Nasi 71
☎ 0923 214 64

CANTINA SICILIANA (€€)

Owner Pino Maggiore is keen to showcase local produce and it's the fish and produce of the *terra* that inspire him. Home-made *busiate* are served with *pesto al trapanese* (tomato, basil, garlic and almond pesto) and fresh swordfish accompanied by tiny tomatoes and capers from Pantelleria.

✉ via Giudecca 36
☎ 0923 28673;
www.cantinasiciliana.it

COLICCHIO (€)

This may be Trapani's best *pasticceria* – superb *cannoli* – but many people come here for the mouth-watering ices, particularly the mulberry, lemon and the different *granite*. There are tables outside.

✉ via delle Arti 6
☎ 0923 547 612

SALT IN THE AIR

All along the coast between Trapani and Marsala are the shallow waters that form Sicily's saltflats, the enclosed pans, glistening, mirror-like, in the sun. Over the course of 80–100 days the water evaporates off, leaving some of Europe's tastiest salt. It is then carted in barrows to be piled in huge heaps, ready for cleaning and packing. You can learn more at the salt museum housed in a 16th-century windmill complex in the depths of the saltflats.

Palermo and the North Coast

PRICES

Expect to pay per double room per night

€ up to €50
€€ = €50–€70
€€€ = €70–€120
€€€€ = over €120

STAYING IN SICILY

Sicily has an excellent cross-section of accommodation, with prices, on the whole, marginally lower than the equivalent on the mainland. Options range from the sybaritic luxury of the grand hotels in Palermo and resorts such as Taormina to family-run, simple *pensione* and private rooms on farms. All types of accommodation are officially graded and the tariff fixed by law. In practice, pricing is more fluid, with mysterious extras hoisting up the price in high season and lower rates available off-season with a little negotiation. On the whole, rooms are abundant in the main towns and tourist areas, but it pays to book ahead in summer or if you're heading inland, where some towns may have very little accommodation.

CEFALÙ

HOTEL ASTRO (€€€)

Clean and simple hotel that's excellent value for money; the staff are exceptionally helpful and friendly and there's the bonus of the hotel's own parking. The beach is five minutes' walk downhill.
✉ via Nino Martoglio 10
☎ 0921 421 639;
www.astrohotel.it

RIVA DEL SOLE (€€€)

Modern hotel overlooking Cefalù beach that's a few minutes' stroll from the old town. Bright and well-equipped, with good accommodation, including sea views and family rooms. No garden or pool.
✉ via Lungomare Giardina 25
☎ 0921 421 230;
www.rivadelsole.com

MONDELLO

ADDAURA (€€€)

Waterfront hotel whose 50 rooms nearly all have sea views and balconies. Two pools, water sports, grounds and a restaurant.
✉ Lungomare Cristoforo Colombo 4452
☎ 091 684 2222;
www.addaura.it

MONREALE

CARRUBELLA PARK (€€)

Hotel set in the hills with spectacular views towards Palermo and sea. Rooms are spacious, clean, comfortable – great value.
✉ via Umberto 1 233, Monreale
☎ 091 640 2187;
www.sicily-hotels.net/CarrubellaParkHotel

PALERMO

CENTRALE PALACE (€€€€)

The Palazzo Tarallo houses this luxurious hotel, decorated with frescoes, stucco work and antique touches; bedrooms veer towards the streamlined with sumptuous bathrooms. Roof garden and excellent restaurant.
✉ Corsa Vittorio Emanuele 327
☎ 091 336 666;
www.centralepalacehotel.it

JOLLY HOTEL DEL FORO ITALICO (€€€)

Big, bland 237-room hotel overlooking the sea with more than adequate rooms and a swimming pool. Good value in this range.
✉ Foro Italico 22
☎ 091 616 5090;
www.jollyhotels.it

LETIZIA (€€–€€€)

A pretty little hotel on a side street with comfortable rooms, some with balconies. All rooms have air conditioning, parquet flooring and public rooms are furnished with antique pieces.
✉ via Bottai 30
☎ 091 589 110;
www.hotelletizia.com

SAUSELE (€)

Friendly hotel that's one of Palermo's best budget deals, with air-conditioned, uncluttered rooms at excellent prices in a safe location near the station. Private parking is available; breakfast extra.
✉ via Vincenzo Errante 12
☎ 091 616 1308;
www.hotelsausele.it

Eastern Sicily

NOTO

HOTEL FERLA (€–€€)

Noto's most up-to-date hotel is on the edge of the historic centre with its own garage. This 15-room hotel has cheery bedrooms with tiled floors; some have balconies. Downstairs all is bright and modern and the garden, planted with olive trees, is a good place to relax.

✉ via a Gramsci 5
☎ 0931 576 007;
www.hotelferla.it

HOTEL JONIO (€–€€)

Ten minutes' drive from the historic town, Noto Marina is a lovely place to stay and this family-run hotel a good find. Set just across the road from the sandy beach, the Jonio has a good dining room and a big terrace; all the rooms have their own balconies.

✉ viale Lido I, Noto Marina
☎ 0931 812 040;
www.hoteljonio.eu

RAGUSA

LOCANDA DON SERAFINO (€€€)

A sensitive restoration has transformed a crumbling 18th-century town house into an intimate, chic and charming boutique hotel whose ten bedrooms combine old-world charm with modern fittings. The Rosa family look after their guests beautifully, are young and enthusiastic and supervise every detail.

✉ via XI Febbraio 15, Ragusa Ibla ☎ 0932 220 065;
www.locandadonserafino.it

IL BAROCCO (€€)

Access to this pretty pink-washed hotel in the heart of Ragusa Ibla is via a courtyard, lovely for relaxing. The rooms, many of which have balconies, are simply and comfortably furnished with good, solid pieces, and have wooden ceilings and cool decor.

✉ via Sta Maria la Nuova 1
☎ 0932 663105;
www.ilbarocco.it

SIRACUSA

DOLCE SILENZIO (€)

Book ahead to stay in the huge attic room, complete with beamed ceiling, of this great budget choice B&B, situated just across the bridge on the island of Ortygia.

✉ via Mirabella 18
☎ 0931 64201;
www.dolcesilenzio.too.it

GRAND HOTEL (€€€€)

Overlooking the Porto Grande, this old palace hotel is grand indeed, with high comfort levels and expert service. Public areas are airy and pleasant, some rooms look out to sea and all guests can enjoy the rooftop restaurant.

✉ viale Mazzini 12
☎ 0931 464 600;
www.grandhotelsr.it

GUTKOWSKI (€€)

The attractive blue-and-white façade gives a taste of what's in store at this friendly and classy hotel, Siracusa's closest to boutique-style. The cool décor of every one of the 25 rooms is imbued with

CHECKING IN AND OUT

If you haven't booked ahead it's quite acceptable to ask to see the room before you decide to book in; remember that if you're travelling with children most hotels will put another bed in the room for an additional one third of the room price. You'll be asked to surrender your passport so the hotel can register you with the police – don't forget to ask for it back. Most 3-star and over hotels accept credit cards; simple *pensione* and B&Bs may not. If you're leaving early, it may make sense to ask to settle the bill the night before you leave. If your departure is after check-out time, many hotels will let you leave your luggage with them until the afternoon.

71

WHAT'S INCLUDED

Hotels in the 3-star and above categories normally include air conditioning and heating in the room price; this may not be the case in budget options. Simpler hotels may also charge extra for breakfast or not offer it at all – in this case, you can have breakfast at a bar just like the Sicilians themselves. Hotel breakfasts are geared to tourists and include a cold buffet with breads, pastries, cold meat and cheese, yoghurt and fruit juices. Luxury hotels will also provide a cooked breakfast. At family-run hotels you may find that staffing levels are minimal, and reception may not be manned 24 hours a day – if you're going to be late back, ask for a key.

sunshine and fresh air, the style simple and elegant.
✉ Lungomare Vittorini 26
☎ 0931 465 861;
www.guthotel.it

HOTEL RELAX (€€)
It may verge on the modern and bland, but there's no denying the comfort of this good-sized hotel near the Neapolis. Bedrooms are big, well equipped and comfortable with plenty of storage, and the hotel is surrounded by lovely grounds and has a wonderful pool.
✉ viale Epipoli 159
☎ 0931 740 122;
www.hotelrelax.it

ROMA (€€€–€€€€)
Built in 1880, this lovely hotel has 44 light and spacious rooms, some with balconies and some equipped for disabled travellers. The hotel restaurant, Vittorini, is among the best in Siracusa.
✉ via Roma 66
☎ 0931 465 626;
www.hotelroma.sr.it

TAORMINA

GRAND HOTEL TIMEO (€€€€)
Taormina's oldest grand-luxe hotel was built in 1873 and is truly everything a luxury hotel should be. Every room is different, all have balconies or a terrace, and the building is surrounded with beautiful gardens. The hotel has a terrace restaurant, pool and health and fitness centre – a real treat.
✉ via Teatro Greco
☎ 0942 23801

PENSIONE SVIZZERA (€€€)
This pretty, pink-washed hotel has been in the same family since 1925, and has its own parking – a real bonus in Taormina – and just 22 rooms making for a cosy stay. Nearly all have a little balcony and views to the sea – the hotel looks northwards.
✉ via Pirandello 26
☎ 0942 23790;
www.pensionesvizzera.com
🕓 Closed Dec–Feb

VILLA GRETA (€€€)
Geraniums and bougainvillea tumble down the balconies of this stepped hotel above the town centre, which has been run by the Lombardo family since 1969. There's a sun-drenched terrace, with views to Etna, and rooms are well equipped, though some are a little on the small side.
✉ via Leonardo da Vinci 46
☎ 0942 28286;
www.villagreta.it

VILLA PARADISO (€€€–€€€€)
With the deep sofas, antique pieces and old prints and pictures, there's more than a touch of the country house style about the public rooms of this lovely hotel. You'll have to pay more for a room with a view, but all 37 have balconies and are nicely furnished; many overlook the garden.
✉ via Roma 2
☎ 0942 23921; www.
hotelvillaparadisotaormina.com
🕓 Mar–Oct

Inland and the South

AGRIGENTO

BAGLIO DELLA LUNA (€€€–€€€€)

Courtyards, a 14th-century tower and rambling old buildings make up this elegant luxury hotel near the Valley of the Temples. De luxe bedrooms, an outside breakfast terrace, a small pool and a renowned restaurant.

✉ Contrada da Maddalusa
☎ 0922 511 061;
www.bagliodellaluna.com

CAMERE A SUD (€)

This is a chic little B&B where your stay will be wonderfully relaxing – and all at year-round excellent prices. Book ahead, and no credit cards.

✉ via Ficani 6
☎ 349 638 4424;
www.camereasud.it

HOTEL AMICI (€–€€)

Bright and modern good value hotel near the station with simple rooms, space to sit outside; some bedrooms have balconies and views down the valley to the sea.

✉ via Acrone 5
☎ 0922 402 831;
www.hotelamici.com

ENNA

BRISTOL (€€)

Opened in 2006, this modern, friendly and good value hotel in the heart of Enna has comfortable and functional rooms; a good budget choice with breakfast included. Parking available.

✉ Piazza Ghisleri 13
☎ 0935 244 15;
www.hotelbristolenna.it

GRAND ALBERGO SICILIA (€€–€€€)

Unprepossessing outside but inside this is a comfortable hotel with big, nicely furnished bedrooms and huge, marble reception area with access to a breakfast terrace. Parking included.

✉ Piazza Napoleone Colajanni 7
☎ 0935 500 850;
www.hotelsiciliaenna.it

PIAZZA ARMERINA IL GIGLIOTTO (€€€)

This is a beautiful family-run *agriturismo* housed in an old monastery with a large pool and pretty gardens. Lovely rooms, excellent restaurant serving estate produce.

✉ SS 117 bis km 60, Piazza Armerina
☎ 0933 970 898;
www.gigliotto.com

OSTELLO DEL BORGO (€)

This a great budget choice with simple, old-fashioned rooms, some with bathrooms; also dormitory-style accommodation. Friendly staff and breakfast included.

✉ Largo San Giovanni 6
☎ 0935 687 019;
www.ostellodelborgo.it

SCIACCA

PENSIONE ALIAI (€)

A stroll from the town centre, this is a comfortable *pensione* with traditionally furnished rooms all overlooking the water; some have tiny terraces.

✉ via Gaie di Garaffe 60
☎ 0925 905 388;
www.aliai.com

BED AND BREAKFAST

There's an increasing number of B&Bs in Sicily, offering good accommodation in private houses at excellent rates. Facilities vary from very upmarket, with pools and lovely gardens, to simple seaside villas, but you can expect clean rooms and a friendly welcome everywhere; many are run by foreigners and specifically cater for non-Italians.

WATCH THAT WATER

Water is scarce in Sicily so, apart from top-end hotels, it's rare to find bath tubs in hotel bathrooms and showers are the norm. Water pressure may vary and the water often merely drains away through a hole in the centre of the bathroom, so don't leave clothes and towels on the floor.

73

Western Sicily

CAMPING

Sicily has over 90 official campsites, mainly around the coast. Most have beaches nearby and facilities will include toilets and showers; more expensive sites may offer swimming pools, tennis courts, shops and restaurants. They are packed in August, when Italians take their holidays, but otherwise uncrowded. Touring Club Italiano (Corso Italia 10, Milan tel 02 852 6245, www.touringclub.it) publishes a campsite guide or check out www.camping.it

PARKING

If you're driving, check ahead to see if your hotel offers parking, a major bonus in towns of any size, and vital in Palermo. If not, aim to drive into town between 1 and 4pm, when streets are quieter and there's some hope of finding a parking space. Never leave anything in your car, take the sound system with you, retract the aerial and turn in the driving mirrors.

ERICE

ELIMO (€€–€€€)

This lovely hotel has wonderful views down to Tràpani and 21 pretty rooms. You can relax in the cosy bar, or sit out on the terrace or in the courtyard. There's an excellent restaurant and private parking.
✉ via Vittorio Emanuele 75
☎ 0923 869 377;
www.hotelelimo.it

MODERNO (€€)

The Moderno has 40 rooms, all well designed. There's a good bar and a terrace with astounding views, but it's the roof terrace restaurant that's the main draw for many guests.
✉ via Vittorio Emanuele 67
☎ 0923 869 300;
www.hotelmodernoerice.it

MARINELLA DI SELINUNTE

MIRAMARE (€€)

Right opposite its own beach, the Miramare's a great choice and very good value, though can be noisy in high season. Front-facing bedrooms have balconies with sea views. The long-established restaurant serves fish straight off the boats.
✉ via Pigafetta 2
☎ 0924 46666;
www.hotelmiramareselinunte.com

SAN VITO LO CAPO

CAPO SAN VITO (€€€–€€€€)

This upmarket, beachside hotel offers everything you'd want for a relaxing stay. The excellent restaurant is candlelit so ideal for a romantic meal.
✉ via Principe Tommaso 29
☎ 0923 972 122;
www.caposanvito.it

MIRASPIAGGIA (€€€)

Miraspiaggia means 'beach view', and this hotel is just across from its private beach, with a fish-speciality restaurant spilling out on to the terrace.
✉ via Lungomare 6
☎ 0923 972 355;
www.miraspiaggia.it

TRAPANI

AI LUMI (€–€€)

Walk off the main street and through a plant-hung courtyard to find Ai Lumi, a friendly bed and breakfast with style. Rooms are simple and elegant, with touches such as antique tables, old tiles and pretty pottery pieces. There are also self-catering, fully equipped apartments.
✉ Corso Vittorio Emanuele 75
☎ 0923 872 418; www.ailumi.it

NUOVO RUSSO (€–€€)

A wonderful survivor of a traditional Sicilian hotel, this family-run place may have old-fashioned rooms but they come with every modern comfort and the public areas are a taste of old Sicily. Breakfast is not included in the room price.
✉ via Tintori 4 ☎ 0923 22166; www.chshotels.com

Ceramics

CEFALÙ

LA TERRA DI PASCAL
Come here to browse among the wonderful selection of colourful ceramics, many of them featuring shapes and designs taken from traditional 18th and 19th century designs. This is a good place to find pottery from Santo Stefano di Camastra, a major ceramic centre just along the coast to the east.
✉ Corso Ruggero 157
☎ 338 485 3423

ERICE

ANTONINO CATALANO
Platters, bowls, jugs and ornamental pottery in all shapes and colours are on offer here, as well as a selection of other typical Sicilian souvenirs.
✉ via Guarnotta 20
☎ 0923 869 126

NOTO

TERRECOTTE
This shop sells some lovely pieces, many featuring traditional shapes and designs – the pots and platters are particularly pretty.
✉ Vicolo Pisacane
☎ 3290 112 365

PALERMO

CERAMICA DE SIMONE
This is the pick of Palermo's ceramic outlets, where you'll find a huge selection of pottery of all kinds, both practical and decorative.
✉ via Lanza di Scalea 960
☎ 091 671 1005

SCIACCA

GASPARE CASCIO
This little shop is piled high with the beautiful deep blue, turquoise and yellow pottery made by local craftsmen. You'll find everything from platters and bowls to cheery ornaments – all at excellent prices so it's a good place to buy souvenirs.
✉ via Vittorio Emanuele 115
☎ 0925 828 29

SIRACUSA

PROVIDENCE
This shop is packed with traditional ceramics – lovely shapes, both decorative and practical, and all decorated with fruit and flower designs.
✉ via Capodieci 55
☎ 0931 22661

TAORMINA

KERAMEION
Climb the steep steps off the Corso to this ceramic studio and shop, where you can watch the craftsmen at work before you buy.
✉ Salita Santippo 16
☎ 0942 239 66

TRAPANI

PERRONE CERAMICHE
This lovely shop sells a wide range of ceramics, including some distinctly quirky designs – the perfectly modelled replicas of traditional food are very tempting as kitchen ornaments.
✉ Corso Vittorio Emanuele 106
☎ 0923 29609

SICILIAN CERAMICS
Sicily has always been renowned for its strong tradition of colourful decorative and practical ceramics, which you'll find for sale wherever you go, though choice is largest and prices best in the pottery towns themselves. Sciacca and Caltagirone are the top producers, with a tradition of high quality pieces as well as everyday ware, and it's also worth checking out Santo Stefano di Camastra on the north coast.

WRAPPED IN STYLE
If you're buying presents, shops in Sicily will gift-wrap purchases for you at no extra cost. Bulky items, such as ceramics can be shipped home, but ensure that the shop offers insurance as part of its service.

Fashion and Jewellery

DEPARTMENT STORES AND MALLS

All Italians prefer personal service to the shopping mall experience and none more so than the Sicilians – so don't expect to find shopping malls as other Europeans know them anywhere in Sicily. Even department stores are very few and far between, Catania and Palermo being the exceptions. Larger towns have branches of chain stores such as Benetton (knitwear and casuals), Intimissimi (underwear) and Feltrinelli (books).

FASHION

AGRIGENTO

POLLINI
Come here if you're looking for shoes – classic and high fashion, comfortable and super-chic are all here, along with a selection of this season's bags and other accessories.
✉ via Atenea 147
☎ 0922 201 70

NOTO

ACETI SANDRINE
Good selection of men's and women's shoes and other leather goods at excellent prices.
✉ via Corradino Sinatra 13
☎ 0931 835 677

PALERMO

BARBISIO COTTONE
Palermo's premier men's outfitters stocks everything the design conscious male could want, from beautifully tailored suits by Versace, Borsalino and Ungaro to casual wear from Missoni, Panicale, Boat House and Paolo da Ponte.
✉ Piazza Marchese di Regalmici 8 ☎ 091 588 774

EMPORIO ARMANI
Like all Armani stores in Italy, this outlet features designs and stock that aren't exported – come here for the best of Italian classic tailoring with style. Prices are a little lower here than in their international stores.
✉ Piazza Antonio Mordini 9
☎ 091 348 654

MAX MARA
This Italian chain is renowned for its seasonal collections of classic women's fashion, beautifully cut and stylish, with a distinctly up-to-the-minute twist.
✉ via Libertà 16/A
☎ 091 588 510

RAGUSA

BATA
This Italian shoe chain sells a wide range of both classic and funky styles for all occasions at excellent prices; bags and belts are also on offer.
✉ Corso Italia 134
☎ 0932 655 530

LA BOUTIQUE ALTA MODA
Lovely women's wear from good designers is found at this shop on Ragusa's best shopping street, with the accent on classy separates.
✉ via Roma 46
☎ 0932 622 908

SIRACUSA

CARPENTIERI
Come here for a good range of leather goods – bags in all shapes and sizes, briefcases, suitcases, wallets and purses.
✉ Corso Matteoti 17/19
☎ 0931 67832

CORTE DEGLI ARANCI
This pretty shop has imaginative and affordable jewellery, made using glass and beads, and lovely scarves, many of them silk hand-blocked.
✉ Corso Matteoti 70
☎ 0931 483 400

KENT

A beautiful shop selling individual and stylish clothes for men and women – the best place to find both classics and elegant up-to-the-minute designs; the staff are particularly friendly.
✉ via Maestranza 23
☎ 0931 68001

SALMOIRAGHI E VIGANO

If you're looking for a bag or wallet, you'll find plenty of choice of supple leather goods here, where classic designs sit side by side with this season's must-haves.
✉ Corso Matteoti 84
☎ 0931 69581

TAORMINA

PARISI

Taormina's best fashion outlet is an elegant store stocking big designer names – come here for famous names such as Versace, Armani, Prada and Dolce e Gabbana.
✉ Corso Umberto I
☎ 0942 231 51

JEWELLERY

ERICE

ALTIERI 1882

This tempting jeweller makes unique and beautiful pieces in gold and coral from nearby Trapani – the earrings and necklaces are mouth-watering. For a cheaper souvenir there's a good selection of vibrant pottery as well.
✉ via Cordici 14
☎ 0923 869 237

PALERMO

GUIDO COSENTINO

A treasure trove of jewellery, silver, crystal and porcelain is to be found in this long-established store.
✉ via Cavour 117
☎ 091 328 362

SIRACUSA

RICCIOLI SALVATORE

This upmarket and expensive jeweller works in gold and silver, using the rare amber found near Siracusa and precious and semi-precious stones.
✉ via dei Mille 3
☎ 0931 65444

TAORMINA

LE COLONNE

The jewellery here is inspired by antique designs and made using old stones and coral – pieces can be made to your own specifications.
✉ Corso Umberto I 164
☎ 0942 625 511

SALVATORE VADALÀ

This is the best of the shops selling coral jewellery – everything from strings of plain beads to ornate brooches.
✉ via Teatro Greco 27
☎ 0942 239 85

TRÀPANI

PLATIMIRO FIORENZA

Coral is traditionally used for jewellery making in this area and you'll find exquisite silver and coral pieces at this fine shop.
✉ via Osorio 36
☎ 0923 438 000

CHOCOLATE!

Look for chocolate in and around Modica, where it's still made as it was in the 16th century when the Spaniards introduced it from Mexico to Sicily, then under their rule. It's dark and grainy and comes flavoured with vanilla, chilli and cinnamon, all Mexican flavourings. The make to look out for is Buonajuto.

Food, Drink and Markets

SICILIAN HONEY

There's a big selection of honey in Sicily and you'll find some of the best in mountain areas, literally for sale beside the road or on offer at local markets. Hives are sited very specifically, producing many single-blossom honeys – look out for thyme, eucalyptus, chestnut flower and orange blossom. Zafferana Etnea is particularly noted for its honey.

WAYSIDE STALLS

If you're driving you'll often see roadside stalls offering fresh produce. These are manned by farmers selling their own produce, which makes the fruit, vegetables, honey and cheese on offer at local markets excellent value and ensuring good quality.

FOOD AND DRINK

CEFALÙ

BACCO ON LINE
This is a serious shop for foodies, where you'll find a great range of Sicilian flavours, ranging from wine from local producers to wonderful liqueurs perfumed with citrus fruit, cinnamon and bay leaves.
✉ Corso Ruggiero 38
☎ 091 421 753

TORREFAZIONE SERIO
Wake up and smell the coffee in this specialist shop, where they will prepare a freshly roasted selection for you – buy the beans or get them to grind and vacuum pack your selection.
✉ Corso Ruggiero 120
☎ 0921 922 348

ENNA

RUSSO FERNANDO
This upmarket and traditional store has Enna's best choice of local cheese and also sells Sicilian liqueurs, among them Ficodì, flavoured with prickly pears, and *digestivi* subtly spiced with cinnamon and citrus.
✉ via Mercato Sant'Antonio 16
☎ 0935 501 031

ERICE

MARIA GRAMMATICO
One of Sicily's most famous *pasticcerie*, where you'll find a superb range of cakes, biscuits and marzipan sweetmeats, all made using centuries-old recipes that were once the guarded secret of Erice's

convents. The beautifully boxed goods make great take-home gifts.
✉ via Vittorio Emanuele 12
☎ 0923 869 672

BAZAR DEL MIELE
This pretty shop is a treasure house for honey lovers, with a huge selection of local honey plus cheeses, fine local olive oil and preserved goods – free tastings of everything are offered.
✉ via Cordici 16
☎ 0923 869 181

MARSALA

STABILIMENTO FLORIO
If you want to buy Marsala direct from the *baglio*, this is the best place to come – you can have a guided tour of the production process and a tasting before you buy.
✉ Lungomare Mediterraneo
☎ 0923 723 846

PALERMO

CAMBRIA
You'll find more than 100 cheeses from all over Sicily at this store, which also sells *salumeria*, oils and pasta. Look out for the *pecorino* (sheep's milk cheese) from Ragusa, the mountain cheeses from the Madonie, as well as a selection of cheeses from mainland Italy.
✉ via Liguria 91
☎ 091 517 791

MANFREDI BARBERA E FIGLI
Founded in 1894, this family-run business produces some of Sicily's finest olive oils. Staff will

be delighted to help you with your choice of the dozens on offer, ranging from light and delicate extra *vergine* (virgin) to wonderfully peppery and aromatic fresh pressed.
- ✉ via E Amari 55/A
- ☎ 091 582 900

RAGUSA

PASTICCERIA LA ROSA
Come here for speciality biscuits, confectionery and chocolate made to the famous recipes from nearby Modica.
- ✉ via Mariannina Schinina' 197
- ☎ 0932 623 086

PUNTO FORMAGGI E SALUMI
A wonderful traditional shop which sells all sorts of *salumeria* and cheese, as well as freshly made sauces and tinned and bottled specialities. The best place to track down an excellent *caciocavallo ragusano*, the local cheese.
- ✉ Corso Italia 32
- ☎ 0923 621 694

SIRACUSA

AGRIFANUSA
The best place in Siracusa for serious food shopping, where you'll find everything from fresh fruit and vegetables to a bewildering selection of tinned and bottled goods.
- ✉ via Adorno 7/B
- ☎ 0931 782 146

TAORMINA

PASTICCERIA ETNA
The lovely old-fashioned interior of this traditional store is the backdrop to

cases filled with the best of local *pasticceria* –they have a huge variety of *frutta di Martorana*.
- ✉ Corso Umberto I 112
- ☎ 0942 247 35

MARKETS

PALERMO

BALLARÒ
Fresh produce, spices, groceries and household goods are on offer.
- ✉ Between Piazza del Carmine and Piazza Ballarò

CAPO
Fresh produce, clothes, household goods, DVDs and cheap jewellery.
- ✉ Between via Sant'Agostino and via Cappuccini

MERCATINO DELLE PULCI
Collectables, second-hand and antique furniture, jewellery and ephemera.
- ✉ via Papireto, near the Cattedrale

VUCCIRIA
Fresh produce, groceries, fish, meat and spices – Palermo's most atmospheric and tourist-friendly market.
- ✉ Between via Roma and Corso Vittorio Emanuele

SIRACUSA

MERCATO
Siracusua's vibrant daily market, with stalls selling fruit and vegetables, fish, cheeses and other foodstuffs, is open in the mornings from Monday to Saturday.
- ✉ Piazza Pancali (near the Tempio di Apollo)

WEEKLY MARKETS

All Sicilian towns of any size have a weekly market on a specified day, when traders roll in and lay out everything from fresh fruit and vegetables, cheeses and *salumeria*, to clothes, household goods and shoes and bags. They're great for a morning's browse and you can soak up the atmosphere and pick up souvenirs to take home – a market visit is an essential part of the Sicilian experience. They operate from 8:30 to around 12:30.

WEIGHTS AND MEASURES

Fruit and vegetables are sold by weight – ask for *un kilo* (a kilo) *un mezzokilo* (a half kilo) or *un'etto* (100 grams). If you're shopping for cheese this is normally sold by the *etto*.

Miscellaneous

BOTTARGA

In western Sicily look out for *bottarga*, the salted dried roe of the tuna fish. It's salted, pressed and then air-dried before packing. Salty, pungent and delicious, it's best sampled grated on home-made pasta as a *primo* – if you see it on the menu, don't miss the chance to taste it and look out for it in good food shops as a souvenir.

ENNA

OPEN SPACE

There's plenty of choice in home accessories at this useful shop, which has both ornamental and practical gifts for the home as well, and stocks a reasonable selection of ceramics.

✉ via Roma 300
☎ 0935 504 701

ERICE

PINA PARISI TAPPETTI

A splendid store selling brightly coloured traditional, hand-made rugs, some woven in geometric patterns, others depicting charming scenes of country life – they are works of art in themselves.

✉ viale Pepoli 55
☎ 0923 869 049

PALERMO

CARNEVALISSIMO

This wonderful shop is devoted entirely to costumes; for babies, kids and adults, with a range of designs from ancient Rome via Disney to Rocky Horror – great fun to browse in even if you don't buy.

✉ via Volturno 33
☎ 091 585 787

LINA D'ANTONA

A marvellously old-fashioned shop with a huge stock of haberdashery – beautiful ribbons and buttons, threads and silks, belts and lace – a delight for crafting enthusiasts.

✉ via Maqueda 413
☎ 091 588 895

MILLENIO IN

This deeply Sicilian speciality shop sells everything you can imagine in the way of party and wedding favours and souvenirs, many of which make great gifts.

✉ Corso Vittorio Emanuele 484
☎ 091 651 2239

SICILY'S FOLK

This famous store sells wonderful hand-carved wooden figures for Christmas nativity cribs pretty enough to serve as ornaments.

✉ Corso Vittorio Emanuele 450
☎ 091 651 2787

SIRACUSA

ISTITUTO DEL PAPIRO

This lovely shop specialises in hand-made paper products, all crafted from the papyrus that grows around Siracusa.

✉ via XX Settembre
☎ 0931 483 342

LA BOTTEGA DEL PUPARO

The hand-carved wooden puppets made here are collector's items; many are copies of traditional characters used in Sicilian puppet theatre. Unique gifts but don't expect bargain prices.

✉ via della Giudecca 17
☎ 0931 465 540

TIFFANY STUDIO AND ART WORKS

This well-known studio a produces artistic glasswork of every type – a good place to pick up something for the home.

✉ via Maestranza 76
☎ 0931 463 649

The Arts, Theatre and Festivals

AGRIGENTO

SAGRA DEL MANDORLO IN FIORE

This festival celebrates the almond blossoming, which signals the arrival of spring. An international folklore festival with performances in town and in the Valley of the Temples. Also parades, feasting, singing, music and puppet shows.
www.mandorloinfiore.net
🕐 Feb

CEFALÙ

CEFALÙ INCONTRI

A mixed arts festival with folklore shows, cabaret and theatre, often staged outside. Occasional performances in the Duomo. Information at the tourist office.
🕐 Jul–Sep

ERICE

ESTATE ERICINA

This summer festival of medieval and Renaissance music holds performances in the Duomo and elsewhere – the tourist office has details.
🕐 Jul–Aug

PALERMO

TEATRO MASSIMO

Palermo's premier arts venue, a grandiose opera house, stages a year-round season of opera, ballet and concerts, with the accent on opera. A performance here would be a highlight of a Sicilian visit.
✉ Piazza Verdi
☎ 091 605 3111;
www.teatromassimo.it

TEATRO POLITEAMA GARIBALDI

This 18th-century theatre is the home of the Orchestra Sinfonica Siciliana, Sicily's symphony orchestra, which performs a year-round series of concerts of classical music.
✉ via Turati 2
☎ 091 588 001

FIGLI D'ARTE CUTICCHIO

This venue offers traditional Sicilian puppet performances – they're in Italian but you don't have to be a linguist to enjoy this unique art. Great family entertainment.
✉ via Bara all'Olivella 95
☎ 091 323 00;
www.figlidartecuticchio.com

KALSART

This is a huge festival of dance, music, theatre and cinema in the Kalsa area, with performances outdoors in some of this atmospheric district's loveliest squares.
www.kalsart.it 🕐 Jul–Sep

U FISTINU DI SANTA ROSALIA

Palermo's, and Sicily's, biggest traditional *festa*, held in honour of the city's patron saint with days of partying, parades, music and fireworks.
🕐 9–15 Jul

FESTAS

Sciacca's Carnival, thought to be the oldest (and best) in Sicily, is celebrated with allegorical floats, music and fireworks.
www.carnevaledisciacca.com
🕐 Feb

NEWSPAPERS

English-language papers are sold in kiosks in Palermo, Catania, Taormina, Cefalù and Siracusa throughout the year, and you may find them elsewhere during the summer months. If you want to browse entertainment listings, pick up a copy of the daily *Il Giornale di Sicilia*.

PUBLIC LAVATORIES

Public toilets are few and far between everywhere in Sicily. The best bet is to use those in museums or head for a restaurant or bar. For the latter, you may have to ask at the counter for the key and it's customary to have a glass of water or *un caffé* if you're using the facilities.

NIGHTLIFE

In summer, club and bar nightlife centres round Mondello, or you could try the side streets off viale della Libertà for classy, posey bars, or head for via Mazzini and via Principe di Belmonte, two pedestrian streets with plenty of outdoor bars.

81

The Arts, Theatre and Festivals

ARETUSA'S SPRING

Siracusa's Fonte Aretusa was one of the most venerated spots in the classical world. The nymph Arethusa was surprised bathing by a river god near Mount Olympus. Fleeing in terror, she reached Siracusa, where the goddess Artemis transformed her into a spring, and the Greeks believed this water was connected with the river in the Peloponnese.

SUMMER FESTIVALS

You can generally pick up tickets for something a couple of days in advance of a performance, but if there's something specific you want to see, book in advance. The websites for the festivals are usually up and running by May and you can book tickets online.

PIAZZA ARMERINA

PALIO DEI NORMANNI
One of Sicily's major medieval *festas*, when knights joust against comers from all over the interior. Competition is fierce and the processions are spectacular.
🕓 12–14 Aug

SAN VITO LO CAPO

COUSCOUS FEST
Cooks flock here from all over the Mediterranean to participate in this wonderfully jolly food festival – every type of couscous is sold, exhibited and cooked, and there are evening parades, fireworks and more.
www.sanvito-couscous.com
🕓 Sep

SIRACUSA

ORTYGIA FESTIVAL
Concerts, plays, dance and exhibitions take place in different venues, either inside or in the open air, all over Ortygia, the ancient heart of the city. Catch a performance under the stars.
www.ortygiafestival.it
🕓 May–Jul

ISTITUTO NAZIONALE DEL DRAMMA ANTICO (INDA)
This highly respected company stages performances of the classical Greek plays, in ancient Greek, at the Teatro Greco and the Anfiteatro Romano in Neapolis. With their innovative productions approach, this company proves that plays written 2,000 years ago still have the power to move the human spirit.
☎ 800 542 6440;
www.indafondazioneorg
🕓 May–July

TAORMINA

TEATRO DEI DUE MARE
The Greek theatre is the setting for performances of classical Greek and Roman plays.
☎ 0942 23243;
www.teatrodeiduemare.it
🕓 Jul–Sep

TAORMINA ARTE
Taormina's biggest arts fest offers a summer season of concerts, theatre and dance at different locations, including the Teatro Greco.
☎ 0942 21142; www.taormina-arte.com 🕓 Jun–Sep

TAORMINA FILMFEST
This film festival runs in conjunction with the other summer arts festivals, with screenings of mainly art-house films from all over the world.
www.taorminafilmfest.it

TRAPANI

ESTATE MUSICALE TRAPANESE
You can enjoy opera in a lovely garden setting at the Villa Margherita during this summer festival; the music society also organises concerts, theatre and dance all year, with visiting orchestras and performers.
☎ 0923 214 54;
www.lugliomusicaletrapanese.it

Sports

DIVING

CEFALÙ

BARAKUDA DIVING CENTER
Equipment for hire and courses for all levels are on offer at this well-equipped dive centre.
✉ Via Cavallero 13

MARSALA

GORGONIA BLU DIVING
A friendly dive school that offers PADI courses and organises dives from their own boats around the Egadi islands. All equipment is available for hire.
✉ via Lipari 20
☎ 347 353 1941;
www.gorgoniablu.it

SAN VITO LO CAPO

ARGONAUTA DIVING CENTER
You can learn how to scuba-dive at this dive centre, which organises day- and week-long courses and both day and night dives for the more experienced. All equipment can be hired.
✉ via Faro 10
☎ 0923 972 888;
www.argonauta-divingcenter.com

TAORMINA

NIKE DIVING CENTRE
You can take a PADI course, learn to take underwater photographs, or simply join a dive at this dive centre below the town.
✉ Località Isola Bella
☎ 3391 961 559;
www.divenike.com

FISHING

CEFALÙ

COOPERATIVA SANTISSIMO SALVATORE-IMBARCAZIONE S GIUSEPPE
Enjoy a day's sea fishing with local fishermen in the waters off the town, then eat your catch on board in the evening.
☎ 3387 551 801

FOOTBALL

PALERMO

Football fans can catch one of Palermo's matches, normally played on Sundays. The team holds its own in the upper ranks of Serie A.
✉ Stadio Renzo Barbera, viale del Fante 11, Palermo
☎ 091 690 1211;
www.ilpalermocalcio.it
💳 (€€) Tickets available online from www.ticketone.it

GOLF

CEFALÙ

LE MADONIE GOLF
This is a well-kept 18-hole course set in the hills with equipment hire and a pro to give advice. Book well ahead and bring proof of your handicap.
✉ Contrada Bartucelli, Collesano
☎ 0921 984 387;
www.lemadoniegolf.com
💳 (€€€)

TAORMINA

IL PICCIOLO
Set in the lovely Gola di Alcantara, this 18-hole

COACH TOURS
If you're in Sicily without a car, there are excursions from the major coastal resorts to the island's best-known classical sites, Mount Etna and Palermo, as well as half-day tours around the resorts – Taormina is best for this, but contact AST.
☎ 095 746 1096, www. aziendasicilianatrasporti.it) for further details.

LATE-NIGHT MANNERS

Sicilians, like most Italians, are abstemious when it comes to alcohol, relying on their natural exuberance for the party spirit. Drunkenness is greatly frowned upon, particularly in remote parts of the interior, so bear in mind that your country may be judged by your personal behaviour.

Sports

DIVING IN SICILY

The waters off Sicily make superb dive sites, particularly in the areas preserved as underwater nature reserves. Many resorts have dive schools offering instruction, but do ensure that they are well-equipped and that safety and tuition levels are to an internationally recognised standard.

LATE-NIGHT SHOPPING

If you don't want to waste precious beach or sightseeing time and you fancy a little after-dinner retail therapy, you'll find that the shops in many resorts are open until around midnight.

course offers some challenging play in verdant surroundings. Booking advised and proof of handicap required. Golf packages available.
✉ via Picciolo, Castiglione di Sicilia ☎ 0942 986 252; www.ilpicciolgolf.com

MOTOR RACING

ENNA

AUTODROMO DI PERGUSA
There are regular Formula 3, Formula 3000 and motorbike races at the circuit surrounding the Lago di Pergusa.
✉ via Nazionale 10, Pergusa ☎ 0935 541 661

RIDING

CEFALÙ

AZIENDA AGRITURISTICA ARIONE
You can stay at this *agriturismo* in the hills of the Madonie or simply book a day's riding. They cater for all levels of expertise and will provide hard hats; very popular in high summer, so book in advance.
✉ Contrada Pozzetti, Collesano ☎ 347 476 37 38; www.agriturismoarione.it

AGRIGENTO

CENTRO IPPICO CONCORDIA
You can go riding at this well-managed riding school, where tuition is also available.
✉ viale Cavaleri Magazzeni 44 ☎ 0922 412 903

SAILING

SIRACUSA

CIRCOLO VELICO ORTIGIA
Organises sailing lessons for both adults and kids.
✉ via Eleorina 95 ☎ 0931 24777

MARSALA

CIRCOLO VELICO MARSALA
Marsala's yacht club hosts summer competitions and also organises boat hire and tuition in small boats.
✉ via Falco 5 ☎ 0923 951 162; www.circolovelicomarsala.com

SWIMMING

ENNA

PISCINA COMUNALE
If you're wilting in the inland heat, you can have a swim at Enna's communal outdoor pool.
✉ Piazzale Onesti, Pergusa ☎ 0935 531 123

TENNIS

SIRACUSA

TENNIS CLUB MATCH BALL
Much more than just a tennis club, this sports centre has two swimming pools and a fitness centre.
✉ via Agnello 26 ☎ 0931 69675

AGRIGENTO

AGRIGENTO TENNIS
Book ahead to play at this complex near Agrigento.
✉ Località Villaseta ☎ 0922 597 272

SICILY
practical matters

WHAT YOU NEED

	UK	Germany	USA	Italy	Spain
● Required ○ Suggested ▲ Not required — Some countries require a passport to remain valid for a minimum period (usually at least six months) beyond the date of entry — contact their consulate or embassy or your travel agent for details.					
Passport/National Identity Card	●	●	●	●	●
Visa (regulations can change — check before you travel)	▲	▲	▲	▲	▲
Onward or Return Ticket	▲	▲	●	▲	▲
Health Inoculations	▲	▲	▲	▲	▲
Health Documentation (reciprocal agreement document: ➤ 90, Health)	●	●	▲	●	●
Travel Insurance	○	○	○	○	○
Driving Licence (national — EU format/national/Italian translation/international)	●	●	●	●	●
Car Insurance Certificate (if own car)	●	●	●	●	●
Car Registration Document (if own car)	●	●	●	●	●

WHEN TO GO

Average figures for Sicily

High season

Low season

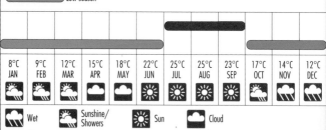

8°C JAN	9°C FEB	12°C MAR	15°C APR	18°C MAY	22°C JUN	25°C JUL	25°C AUG	23°C SEP	17°C OCT	14°C NOV	12°C DEC

Wet   Sunshine/Showers   Sun   Cloud

TIME DIFFERENCES

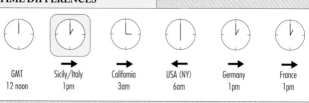

GMT 12 noon	Sicily/Italy 1pm	California 3am	USA (NY) 6am	Germany 1pm	France 1pm

TOURIST OFFICES

In the UK
Italian National Tourist Office
1 Princes St
London W1R 8AY
☎ 020 7408 1254

In the USA
In the USA
Italian National Tourist Office
630 Fifth Avenue, Suite
1565, New York NY 10111
☎ 212/245-5168

Websites
• Italian State Tourist Board:
www.enit.it
• Sicilian Regional Tourist Board:
www.regione.sicilia.it/turismo
• Italian National Parks:
www.parks.it

ARRIVING

Palermo Airport
Kilometres to city centre

31 kilometres

Journey times

🚌	60 minutes
🚐	70 minutes
🚗	45 minutes

Catania Airport
Kilometres to city centre

5 kilometres

Journey times

🚌	N/A
🚐	20 minutes
🚗	15 minutes

Ferry from Reggio Calabria
Kilometres to Messina

5 kilometres

Journey times

🚢	35 minutes
🚢	15 minutes

TIME

Sicily is one hour ahead of Greenwich Mean Time (GMT) in winter, and one hour ahead of BST in summer, six hours ahead of New York and nine hours ahead of Los Angeles. Clocks are advanced one hour in March and turned back in October.

CUSTOMS

YES

From another EU country for personal use (guidelines)
800 cigarettes
200 cigars
1 kilogram of tobacco
10 litres of spirits (over 22%)
20 litres of aperitifs
90 litres of wine, of which 60 litres can be sparkling wine
110 litres of beer

From a non-EU country for your personal use, the allowances are:
200 cigarettes OR
50 cigars OR
250 grams of tobacco
1 litre of spirits (over 22 %)
2 litres of intermediary products (eg sherry) and sparkling wine
2 litres of still wine
50 grams of perfume
0.25 litres of eau de toilette

The value limit for goods is €240

Travellers under 17 years of age are not entitled to the tobacco and alcohol allowances.

NO

Drugs, firearms, ammunition, offensive weapons, obscene material, unlicensed animals.

MONEY

The euro (€) is the official currency of Italy. Euro coins are issued in denominations of 1, 2, 5, 10, 20 and 50 euro cents and €1 and €2. Notes are issued in denominations of €5, €10, €20, €50, €100, €200 and €500. Foreign currency and traveller's cheques can be changed at banks and exchange bureaux *(cambio)*, and you can withdraw cash from ATM (cashpoint) machines using your credit or debit card and a PIN (personal identification number). Major credit cards *(carta di credito)* are accepted in larger hotels, restaurants and shops, though cash is preferred in remote places and smaller establishments.

CONSULATES

UK	Ireland	USA	Canada	Australia
☎ 091 326 412	☎ 06 697 9121	☎ 091 305 857	☎ 06 854 441	☎ 06 852 721

TOURIST OFFICES

Palermo
Piazza Castelnuovo 35
☎ 091 583 847/091 605 8111;
www.palermotourism.com
🕔 Mon–Fri 8:30–2, 3–7, Sat 9–1

Agrigento
via Cesare Battisti 15
☎ 0922 204 54;
www.agrigento-sicilia.it

Cefalù
Corso Ruggiero 77
☎ 0921 421 050;
www.cefalu-tour.pa.it;
www.cefaluinforma.it

Enna
via Roma 413
☎ 0935 528 288;
www.apt-enna.com

Erice
via Tommaso Guarrisi 1
☎ 0923 869 388;
www.apt.trapani.it/Erice (Italian only)

Marsala
via XI Maggio 100
☎ 0923 714 097/993 270;
www.lagunablu.org

Noto
Piazzale XVI Maggio
☎ 0931 896 654/0931 573779;
www.comune.noto.sr.it (Italian only)

Siracusa
via della Maestranza 33 (Ortygia)
☎ 0931 464 255;
www.apt-siracusa.it

Taormina
Palazzo Corvaja, Piazza Vittorio
Emmanuele
☎ 0942 23243;
www.gate2taormina.com

NATIONAL HOLIDAYS

J	F	M	A	M	J	J	A	S	O	N	D
2		(1)	1(1)	1	1		1			1	3

1 Jan	New Year's Day
6 Jan	Epiphany
Mar/Apr	Easter Monday
25 Apr	Liberation Day
1 May	Labour Day
2 Jun	Republic Day
15 Aug	Ferragosto (Feast of the Assumption)
1 Nov	All Saints' Day
8 Dec	Feast of the Immaculate Conception
25 Dec	Christmas Day
26 Dec	St Stephen's Day

OPENING HOURS

○ Shops	● Pharmacies
● Offices	● Museums/Monuments
● Banks	● Churches

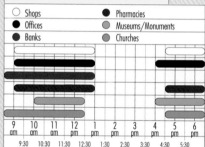

9 am	10 am	11 am	12 pm	1 pm	2 pm	3 pm	4 pm	5 pm	6 pm
	9:30	10:30	11:30	12:30	1:30	2:30	3:30	4:30	5:30

Shops: In general Tue–Sat 8–1, 4:30–8, though food shops are also open on Mondays as are shops in holiday resorts. Shops in larger towns and cities may be open all day (*orario continuato*)
Banks: Generally banks are open 8:30–1:20 and 3–4.
Post offices: Mon–Sat 8:30–6:30 at main branches, shorter hours and Saturday closing in provincial areas.
Museums and churches: Generally 9–1 and 4–6, but this can vary and many are closed on Monday or at the whim of the custodians.
Archaeological sites are open from 9 until an hour before sunset.
Pharmacies: They are usually open 8–1, 2–7, but duty chemists will be open 24 hours on a rota system.

ELECTRICITY

The power supply is 220 volts AC.

Sockets take two-pronged round continental plugs. Visitors from the UK will need an adaptor, and visitors from the USA will need a transformer for 100–120 volt devices.

TIPS/GRATUITIES

Yes ✓   No ✗

Restaurants (service included)	✗	discretionary
Cafés/bars (service included)	✗	discretionary
Taxis	✓	round up
Tour guides	✓	discretionary
Hotels	✗	
Porters	✓	€1 per bag
Chambermaids	✓	€1 per night
Hairdressers	✓	€2–€3
Restroom attendants	✓	change

PUBLIC TRANSPORT

 Domestic flights Both Catania Fontanarossa (☎ 800 56 56 60, flight information ☎ 095 340 505; www.aeroporto.catania.it) and Palermo Falcone Borsellino (☎ 800 541 880/091 702 0111, airport information ☎ 091 702 0273; www.gesap.it) airports handle domestic flights from other Italian cities.

 Trains Sicily has a good train network, which passes through all the main centres, though services can be slow. The fastest trains are Intercity, for which a supplement is payable. The coast is better served than the interior and some stations can be a distance away from the town they serve. Fares are low and trains usually on time. You can check timetables and book tickets on-line at www.ferroviedellostato.it

 Buses Sicilian buses (*autobus* or *pullman*) cover everywhere you'll want to go and are reliable, comfortable and often air-conditioned. Bear in mind that services are drastically reduced, or even non-existent, on Sunday and that timetables on some out-of-the-way routes are geared to the school day or local markets, making departure times horribly early. Bus terminals (*autostazione*) can be scattered all over the bigger towns; in smaller places buses stop in a main piazza or outside the railway station. Timetables are available online, from company offices, bus stations or on the bus. Buy tickets on board or in advance from company offices. City buses are cheap and frequent; buy tickets at *tabacchi* or from kiosks before you board and validate them in the machine on the bus.

Main Bus Operators
AST (☎ 095 746 1096; www.aziendasicilianatrasporti.it)
Interbus (☎ 095 532 2716; www.interbus.it)
SAIS Trasporti (☎ 095 536 6168; www.saistrasporti.it)

CAR RENTAL

All the major international firms have outlets at both Catania and Palermo airports and in the cities, though it may be cheaper to arrange a deal before you leave home. Note that the car hire desks at Catania are in a building opposite Arrivals.

TAXIS

 Taxis operate in Palermo and most other Sicilian towns of any size. They are normally green-and-white or cream and display an illuminated taxi sign; pick them up from taxi ranks. Be sure to check that the meter is properly set at the start of your journey.

CONCESSIONS

Student holders of an International Student Card (ISIC) or an International Youth Card (IYC) can take advantage of discounts on transport and museum entrance fees, as well as being eligible to stay at youth hostels and other concessionary accommodation. Nationals (under 18) of EU and certain other countries receive free admission to state museums.

Senior citizens aged over 65 of EU and other countries with which Italy has a reciprocal arrangement (not including the USA) may gain free admission to some museums and reductions on public transport on production of their passport.

DRIVING

 Speed limit on motorways **130kph (80mph)**

 Speed limit on main roads **110kph (68mph)**

 Speed limit in towns **50kph (31mph)**

 Seat belts are compulsory for all passengers. Children under 4 must have a suitable restraint system. Those aged 4–12 cannot travel in the front seat without a fitted restraint.

 There are severe penalties for drink driving; the legal level is below 0.05 per cent.

 Unleaded petrol (*senza piombo*) is the norm. Petrol stations on *autostrada* (motorways) are open 24/7 and take credit cards, as do larger stations in towns. Petrol is available from automatic dispensers 24/7 at stations in towns and on main roads. In rural areas petrol stations are normally shut on Sundays.

 Hired cars and their drivers should be insured by the hire company. In the event of a breakdown, call the hire car company's emergency number. Driving in Palermo and Catania is traumatic for foreigners unused to Sicilian driving and best avoided if possible. Elsewhere, drivers should be constantly alert. Dipped headlights should be used at all times outside built-up areas.

PHOTOGRAPHY

 What to photograph: There are endless photographic subjects all over Sicily ranging from superb mountains, landscape and coastline to cities, classical sites and colourful markets. In summer, the light is very strong in the middle of the day, so morning and late afternoon is the best time for photography.

PERSONAL SAFETY

Violence against tourists is unusual in Sicily, but petty crime such as pickpocketing and bag snatching and theft from cars is common.

● Do not wear or display expensive equipment or jewellery.
● Always lock valuables in hotel safety deposit boxes
● Never leave anything inside your car. If you have to, lock it out of sight in the boot.
● Beware of pickpockets in crowded markets and busy streets
● Use common sense and stick to well lit streets at night
● Carry shoulder bags slung across your body

Police assistance:
☎ **112**
from any call box

TELEPHONES

There are numerous Telecom Italia public telephones on the street and in Telecom Italia offices. They take coins, credit cards and phonecards (*schede telefoniche*); these are on sale at newsstands and *tabacchi* (tobacconists). Tear the corner off the card before use. You can also send a text from a public telephone. International calls are cheaper between 10 pm and 8 am Mon–Fri and all day Sunday. Calls from hotel rooms will invariably attract a heavy premium.

International Dialling Codes
Dial 00 followed by
UK:	44
USA/Canada:	1
Irish Republic:	353
Australia:	61

POST

Post Offices
Stamps (*francobolli*) can be bought at tobacconists, post offices and some gift shops in tourist resorts. Letters to European Union countries should arrive within 5–7 days, and to the USA within 10 days. Send urgent mail by *posta prioritaria* and ensure that you post it in a blue post box. Other post boxes are red.

HEALTH

Insurance
Citizens of EU countries receive reduced-cost emergency health care with relevant documentation (European Health Insurance Card), but private medical insurance is still advised and essential for all other visitors. Ask at your hotel for details of English-speaking doctors.

Dental Services
Dental treatment is not covered by the health service and you will have to pay for treatment, but your insurance should cover the costs.

Weather
The sun can be intense at all times of year, and it is possible to burn very quickly. Cover up with high-factor sunscreen, wear a hat and drink plenty of water, especially if walking in the hills or along the coast. If you sleep with the windows open, insect repellent and an electrical mosquito zapper may be useful.

Drugs
Chemists (*farmacie*) are open Mon–Sat 9–1 and 4–8. Some open through lunch and the late-night duty chemist is posted in pharmacy windows. Pharmacists are highly trained and can sell some drugs that require prescriptions in other countries. However, take adequate supplies of any drugs you take regularly as they may not be available.

Safe Water
Tap water is safe but most people drink mineral water. Ask for sparkling (*gassata* or *frizzante*) or still (*naturale* or *liscia*) bottled water.

LANGUAGE

Italian is a relatively easy language to learn – particular combinations of letters are generally pronounced the same way. The stress is usually on the penultimate syllable, but if the word has an accent, this is where the stress falls. All Italian nouns are either masculine (usually ending in o when singular or i when plural) or feminine (usually ending in a when singular or e when plural). Some nouns, which may be masculine or feminine, end in e (which changes to i when plural). An adjective's ending changes to match the ending of the noun.

hotel	albergo	how much per night?	quanto costa una notte?
single room	singola		
double room	matrimoniale	double/single room	camera doppia/singola
reservation	prenotazione	with bath/shower	con bagno/doccia
room service	servizio nella stanza	when is breakfast served?	a che ora è servita la colazione?
toilet	gabinetto		
do you have a room?	avete camere libere?		

bank	banca	cheque	cheque
exchange office	cambio	traveller's cheque	traveller's cheque
post office	ufficio postale	credit card	carta di credito
coin	moneta	exchange rate	corse del cambio
banknote	banconote		

café	caffè	beer	birra
waiter	cameriere	wine	vino
waitress	cameriera	water	acqua
bill	conto	coffee	caffè

airport	aeroporto	boat	battello
train	treno	ticket	biglietto
station	stazione	single ticket	andante
bus	autobus	return ticket	andante e ritorno
bus stop	fermata d'autobus	car	machina

what is the time?	che ore sono	I'm sorry	mi dispiace
when do you open/close?	a che ora apre/chiude?	where is the train/ bus station?	dov'è la stazione ferroviaria/degli autobus?
I don't speak Italian do you speak English?	non parlo italiano parla inglese?		
I don't understand	non capisco	where are we?	dove siamo?
what does this mean?	cosa significa questo?	do I have to get off here?	devo scendere qui?
my name is	mi chiamo	how much is this?	quanto costa questo?
what's your name?	come si chiama?	I'm looking for...	cerco...
hello, pleased to meet you	piacere	where can I buy...?	dove posso comprare...?
I'm here on holiday	sono qui in vacanza	help!	aiuto!
good morning	buongiorno	can you help me, please?	può aiutarmi, per favore?
good afternoon/evening	buona sera		
goodbye	arrivederci	I have lost my passport/wallet	ho perso il passaporto/il portafoglio
see you later	a più tardi		
see you tomorrow	a domani	where is the police station?	dov'è il commissariato?
see you soon	a presto	where is the hospital?	dov'è l'ospedale?
how are you?	come sta?	I don't feel well	non mi sento bene
fine, thank you	bene, grazie		

REMEMBER

- Confirm your flight the day before departure.

- Arrive 2 hours before your scheduled flight departure time. Ensure that you have all necessary documentation ready. Check on goods allowed in hand luggage.

- Allowances for exporting goods vary with destination – check before departure.

Index

TwinPack
Sicily

Written by Sally Roy
Verfified by Mary McLean
Produced by AA Publishing
Project editor Karen Rigden
Designer Jacqueline Bailey
Series editor Cathy Hatley

A CIP catalogue record for this book is available from the British Library.

ISBN 978-0-7495-5715-7

Published by AA Publishing, a trading name of Automobile Association Developments Limited, whose registered office is Fanum House, Basing View, Basingstoke, Hampshire, RG21 4EA. Registered number 1878835.

© **AUTOMOBILE ASSOCIATION DEVELOPMENTS LIMITED 2008**
First published 2008

Colour separation by Keenes, Andover
Printed and bound by Everbest Printing Co. Limited, China

ACKNOWLEDGEMENTS
The Automobile Association would like to thank the following photographers, companies and picture libraries for their assistance in the preparation of this book. Abbreviations for the picture credits are as follows: (t) top; (b) bottom; (l) left; (r) right; (AA) AA World Travel Library.

9 N Setchfield/Alamy; 26t CuboImages srl/Alamy; 26b CuboImages srl/Alamy; 27t Getty Images; 37t CuboImages srl/Alamy; 59 D Delimont/Alamy; 87 European Central Bank.

The remaining photographs are held in the Automobile Association's own photo library (AA World Travel Library) and were all taken by Neil Setchfield with the exception of:

5t, 12b, 20r, 23t, 33t, 33b, 39t, 44b, 46t, 52, 61b, 90tr by Clive Sawyer; 12t by Anna Mockford & Nick Bonetti; 58 by Simon McBride; 90br by Max Jourdan.

Front cover: top–bottom, left–right; (a) AA/N Setchfield; (b) AA/N Setchfield; (c) AA/C Sawyer; (d) AA/N Setchfield (e) AA/N Setchfield; (f) AA/N Setchfield; (g) AA/N Setchfield; (h) AA/N Setchfield; F/C b/g AA/C Sawyer; B/Ca AA/N Setchfield; B/Cb AA/C Sawyer; B/Cc AA/N Setchfield; B/Cd Brand X Pics.

Every effort has been made to trace the copyright holders, and we apologise in advance for any accidental errors. We would be happy to apply the corrections in the following edition of this publication.

AO3016
Mapping in this title produced from map data © New Holland Publishing (South Africa) (Pty) Ltd. 2007.

TITLES IN THE TWINPACK SERIES
• Algarve • Andalucía • Corfu • Costa Blanca • Costa Brava • Costa del Sol • Crete •
• Croatia • Cyprus • Dubai • Gran Canaria • Lanzarote & Fuerteventura • Madeira •
• Mallorca • Malta & Gozo • Menorca • Provence & the Côte d'Azur • Sardinia • Tenerife •